Straight
Down
the
Middle

Straight Down the Middle

Shivas Irons, Bagger Vance,
and How I Learned to Stop Worrying
and Love My Golf Swing

JOSH KARP

CHRONICLE BOOKS
SAN FRANCISCO

Library of Congress Cataloging-in-Publication Data is available.

ISBN: 978-0-8118-6359-9

Manufactured in Canada
Designed by Jacob T. Gardner
Typeset in Bembo and Trade Gothic
10 9 8 7 6 5 4 3 2 1

Chronicle Books LLC
680 Second Street
San Francisco, CA 94107
www.chroniclebooks.com

For Susan

TABLE OF CONTENTS

———————◦———————

———————◦———————

Why is it that thousands of people are now having these mini-satori experiences playing golf? That's fascinating in its own right. People who've never heard of satori, who've never even heard of Zen, who have no spiritual aspiration whatsoever—all these guys out there having spiritual experiences. I think that golf is a mystery school for Republicans.

—GOLF IN THE KINGDOM AUTHOR MICHAEL MURPHY

———————○———————

That was a great game of golf, fellas.

—BING CROSBY'S LAST WORDS

Introduction:
The Worst Club in My
Bag Is My Brain

They say golf is like life, but don't believe them.
Golf is more complicated than that.

—GARDNER DICKINSON

They say that every journey begins with the first step. This was mine.

A friend of my wife's once commented that I appeared to be a "new soul." This, I was smart enough to realize, was to be contrasted with an "old soul," which ostensibly is someone who has been here before and learned the lessons of the world and of life. An old soul has accrued wisdom.

New souls? Well, we're another matter completely. Couched in a term that makes us sound open and innocent, the truly enlightened understand this comment to refer to someone whose brain is filled with inconsequential batting averages and memories of long-forgotten episodes of *The White Shadow*. New souls lack depth. We are free of existential ennui. The comment, though made in good cheer, was a way of saying that

I was a banal, happy-go-lucky suburban doofus who loves golf, steak, and Patrick Swayze movies.

Well, I don't much like Patrick Swayze movies. I mean *Roadhouse* aside. And *Point Break*. But I get where she was coming from. I am not someone who seems to be pondering the imponderable, and above all else I most likely appear to be a relentless seeker of comfort, the creation of which has been my primary purpose for as long as I can remember. In the world of old souls, I suppose I seem unconcerned with anything that is happening beyond the sports section of my newspaper.

Never was my "new soul" more staggeringly apparent than during a meditation seminar at Chicago's Shambhala Center where, in a room filled with enlightened beings, I was clearly the only one who'd hugged a complete stranger in the men's room moments after the White Sox beat Houston in Game Two of the 2005 World Series.

That evening we sat in a circle for several hours, quietly observing our breath and trying to "effortlessly" observe our thoughts, while letting them drift away like clouds against a clear blue sky. I found the exercise damn near impossible.

Now, I wasn't new to meditation. Instead, after having been introduced to the practice by a somewhat New Agey friend the year before, I'd been trying to meditate for at least ten minutes most days, hoping to clear the anxious cobwebs from my addled brain. Because underneath my seemingly mellow exterior are gut-churning angst and fears that range from disease to a cataclysmic plane crash to financial ruin.

Sitting there, I would breathe in—and think about the crap I needed to do around the house—and then out. I would breathe in—consider some new and undetected cancer—and breathe out. If there were any clouds blowing across my sky, they looked like black tornadoes.

During a silent break, with my back aching and my mind filled with murderous thoughts toward my fellow aspiring Buddhists (I tried unsuccessfully to let them pass like clouds), I turned away from the herbal tea and vegan baked goods that had been laid out before us and began to wonder how I might lure my wife off to dinner and a movie.

But I was too late. We were called back to the meditation room where our leader, a small, serene software executive named Bob, said we would go around the circle discussing what we had observed or learned from our practice.

As we began, everyone was very clear that we were not to mention goals or ambitions. That kind of practical, purpose-driven stuff is not the point of Zen Buddhism. Instead, even I knew that you meditated because it was what you did—a part of your life. It was "practice"—the practice of returning to your breath, the practice of letting go of your attachment to your thoughts. You meditated to gain greater intimacy with yourself and to be in the present moment, like Thoreau sitting in his doorway at Walden watching the sunlight play on the floor from dawn until night fell.

When others spoke, it seemed that they were getting closer to their true selves. Some had accessed anger they didn't know existed (never a problem for me). Others had become imperceptibly, but definitely, more present.

Then it was my turn: I discussed how meditation had improved my golf game. I mentioned how I got over bad shots more quickly. I said that I'd learned to let go of my score a bit and, strangely enough, how doing so had helped me drop a stroke or two.

I glanced around the room only to see my wife shaking her head in resigned recognition, while enlightened smiles turned to sneers of nonjudgmental derision that apparently arise when a "new soul" gets all purposeful about their meditation.

Bob looked at me warmly. He smiled. And then said, "The Sakyong is an avid golfer."

The Sakyong is Sakyong Mipham Rinpoche, the leader of Shambhala and a pretty interesting guy. Author, calligrapher, horseman, poet, and marathon runner, he is something of a Buddhist renaissance man, whose father, Trungpa Rinpoche, is widely credited with bringing Buddhism to the West. A few years older than me, Sakyong Mipham is said to be the reincarnation of Mipham the Great, which I believe is a pretty heavy credential in the world of Zen.

Before that evening I knew quite a bit about the Sakyong, had read part of one of his books, and considered him an all-around fascinating and admirable guy. Now, however, I knew that he was a golfer and was perhaps as close to a Dalai Lama with a gap wedge as I might ever find.

I'm not ashamed to admit that my mind wandered in that moment. I began to have visions of myself and the Sakyong—flowing robes, the whole bit—teeing it up at some mystical golf course where he would help me learn to quiet my mind, achieve inner peace, and lower my handicap in the process. By the time we left the Shambhala Center that evening, I had decided that I was ready to go on a quest.

The quest. My quest, the quest that became this book, was one toward two goals—better golf and a better life via the non-traditional Eastern route. I would sample various Eastern approaches to golf and life—meditation, martial arts, and all other manner of instruction both on the course and off—hoping to lower my handicap and find my true, calm, happy self, or vice versa.

I knew that my journey was bound to be filled with false starts, pitfalls, and facing up to the demons that haunt my golf game and my inner life. But I also knew that golf was a legitimate vehicle toward greater self-knowledge. Many have gone before me, and they've written books about it. I've read nearly every golf-meets-spirituality novel, how-to, and memoir out there. I've read *Zen Golf, Extraordinary Golf,* and *Fearless Golf.* I've read Harvey Penick's *Little Red Book* and Kjell Enhager's *Quantum Golf.* If somebody with a book deal has learned the meaning of life while playing Pinehurst, chances are the book is sitting on my bookshelf.

But the true heart of this quest lies in two books—*The Legend of Bagger Vance* and *Golf in the Kingdom.* The latter, published in 1972, is what Keith Jackson might call "the granddaddy of them all."

For the uninitiated, *Golf in the Kingdom* is Michael Murphy's novel in the guise of a fictionalized memoir of his stopover in Scotland while on his way to an ashram, during which he encounters a shamanic golf pro named Shivas Irons at the mythical Burningbush links. During roughly a twenty-four hour period they play eighteen holes, then undertake a semi-drunken all-night exploration of golf's relationship to ancient history, Eastern philosophy, religion, quantum physics, and the meaning of life. The book is a brilliant ramble that—like most great novels of this nature—fails to tie things up neatly, instead leaving the reader with as many questions as it does answers. The story has a beginning, middle, and end but, in essence, is a treatise on the larger meaning of golf. It is fascinating and occasionally incomprehensible. It is also the best-selling golf book of all time.

Before Murphy's book, golf was Jack and Arnie. It was plaid pants, a wood-paneled station wagon, and Scotch on a Sunday afternoon, set to the comforting tones of Pat Summerall.

But, Murphy—a key figure in the Human Potential Movement of the 60s and 70s (as well as a founder of the Esalen Institute in Big Sur)—took that bland suburban game and slyly merged it with a bit of mysticism, nontraditional spirituality, and self-help, all of which would gain momentum as the baby boomers cut their hair and became just like their parents.

Before long, golf wasn't just golf. Instead, it was a metaphor for life, with every fairway leading to heaven and every green a mirror into which man gazed and saw his true self staring back. Golf was metaphysical, existential, and shrouded in the kind of strained symbolic thinking that generally fills me, at best, with derisive bile. The answers, I have always believed, are not really out there—and if they are, then I suspect that they haven't been unlocked by people who appear on *Oprah* (yes, you, Eckhart Tolle) or write best-selling golf books.

At the same time, however, I also saw something quite genuine within the "golf is life, life is golf" movement. It is what I realized when meditation started improving my game. I hadn't taken a lesson or changed my swing. Nor had I purchased a new putter or gigantic titanium driver. Instead, I was just a bit more present when I played, a bit less focused on the end result, and a bit more in tune with the journey. And within all of that I began to believe that there was possibly something deeper happening when I walked the fairways.

Shortly after the meditation seminar, I rented Robert Redford's adaptation of Steven Pressfield's *The Legend of Bagger Vance*, which is a retelling of the *Bhagavad Gita* set against a fictional golf match in the South during the era of Bobby Jones and Walter Hagen. Played by Will Smith, Bagger ("Bagger Vance" represents "Bhagavad," which means the "divine one") is an earthy, wise caddy who comes to assist Matt Damon's Rannulph Junuh (Arjuna is the protagonist of the *Bhagavad Gita*), a former golf champion who lost his true self while fighting in World War I. Returning home, he becomes a drunken layabout, until he is forced to play a match against Jones and Hagen. But it turns out that when he lost his true self, his "authentic swing" disappeared along with it—which could explain the need to get drunk all the time. Luckily, Bagger helps him relocate both his authentic swing and his true self—which are in some ways one and the same.

This is how Bagger explains the "authentic swing" at one point during Junuh's struggle against the golfing gods: "It's something we was born with. Something that's ours and ours alone. It's something that can't be learned. It's something that's gotta be *remembered*."

A cynic at heart, I am disinclined to believe in such phenomena. But there is also someone inside of me who realizes that all that stands between myself, a lower handicap, and inner peace can be found in something that Shivas Irons says to Michael Murphy: "You try too hard and think too much."

Indeed I do both to excess. Which led me to realize it was now or never. If I was going to find that authentic swing of mine, or find out if such a thing really existed, I needed to make the journey.

Thus, despite my grave and serious doubts about this concept or the idea that a normal American man could search for inner peace without giving up his perfectly reasonable hatred of the Chicago Cubs, I decided to head off on a quest to find my authentic swing and true self, using the fairways and greens as my Walden Pond—much to the envy of other men, and to the dismay of my wife.

During the nearly two years between January of 2007 and October of 2008, I planned to transform my life and my 18-handicap golf game from the inside out. Rather than tinkering with my equipment or going to see Hank Haney, I would undertake a strict regimen of nontraditional, Eastern-inspired instruction. I would take lessons based in the martial arts, yoga, Zen Buddhism, and anything else that mixed mysticism and the Masters. Then, with my game transformed, I would head off to play with various mystics, shamans, and men of the cloth, hoping to locate my authentic swing while sorting the charlatans from the would-be Shivas Ironses, Bagger Vances, and Dalai Lamas.

The end result, I hoped, would be a new me. A man who, at forty, was approaching the back nine of life with an enviable golf game and a newfound sense of self, free of my frequent anxieties about untimely death—and even the timely variety. I set off to determine whether this golf-and-spirituality stuff was legitimate, or just a good way to sell books to middle-aged guys with a golf jones. My goal, I decided, was to accept my demise and get rid of my inner Woody Allen by channeling my inner Bing Crosby. And no, I'm not talking about the Bing Crosby accused of using corporal punishment on his children any more than the legions of Sinatra worshippers endorse alcoholism, blinding rage, mob connections, and tossing the occasional stranger through a plate glass window. No, I'm talking about the Bing Crosby we know and love, the happy-go-lucky 2-handicap who neither tried too hard nor thought too much. Simply put, a normal, laid-back, self-effacing, anxiety-free American guy with a great golf game and not a care in the world.

As I planned this journey into both myself and a world where golf and spirituality are one and the same, I remembered something my wife's friend said when she found out I was considering this quest. Despite having never picked up a club in her life, she looked at me with a bemused expression and said, "It's no mystery why people think life mirrors the game of golf. You play against yourself and you can never win."

Part One

OUT

CHAPTER I

Things to Do in Denver When You're an 18-Handicap

God is pleased with the work that I do.
In some ways, I'm very much like God.

—MOSHE FELDENKRAIS

WINTER 2007. DENVER, COLORADO

Perhaps we should begin here. I love effortlessness. In fact, I'm all about effortlessness. Effortlessness is the central tenet of my personal philosophy, and if you equate effortlessness with lack of effort, there are many (parents, high school teachers, wife, former employers) who think I achieved it long ago.

And thus, at the outset of my quest, I became immediately interested when I saw the words "effortless swing" on Yoni Zaluski's Web site for Whole Body Golf, which integrates the mechanics of the golf swing with the principles of Feldenkrais, a method of movement therapy that combines body and breath awareness to improve function and increase range of motion. The end result: greater power, and with ah-less effort.

Yoni and I emailed. We talked. We shared our interest in golf and nontraditional golf instruction. But, in truth, like Renee Zellweger in *Jerry Maguire*, Yoni had me at "effortless." We decided that I should come to Denver.

o o o o

Yoni picks me up one cold winter morning at my hotel near the airport. At fifty-four, he is lean and intense, bearing a striking resemblance to a closely shorn Michael Bolton—with a fading Israeli accent.

Both a certified Feldenkrais practitioner and a licensed golf instructor, Yoni brought the two disciplines together after wrecking his back ten years ago. When no traditional or alternative therapy seemed to work, a friend suggested that Yoni try Feldenkrais. After two sessions with a practitioner, Yoni's pain was dramatically reduced. A successful engineer with money in the bank, he quickly decided—in one of those man-meets-mission stories—that he would fuse his love for golf with his belief in the power of Feldenkrais.

As we drive through suburban Denver on our way to Yoni's office, we discuss golf, the body-mind connection, and the failings of traditional instruction. Before long we realize that both of us have recently read a book entitled *Tour Tempo*.

"I don't want to be negative," Yoni begins, "but [*Tour Tempo*] forces a certain rhythm and coordination on you. We all have our own rhythm: Tiger, Ernie, you, me—we're all different."

This will not be the last time that Yoni tells me that he "doesn't want to be negative," or that he is "getting negative" about mainstream golf instruction. I've had enough therapy to recognize that he's working on himself and trying to be a better person. I'm actually doing the same after reading the Dalai Lama's *How to Practice*, whose hundreds of pages can be boiled down to the central message, "Don't be negative."

Though this shared desire to avoid a corrosive emotion seems like Kismet, I tell him it's okay and quietly encourage further negativity. It's an old habit.

Yoni and I agree that most instructional books and lessons are geared towards our quick-fix culture, with every student feeling cheated if they aren't measurably better or cured during each lesson. Even worse, we both say, are the endless streams of specific instructions ("left arm straight," "right arm bent," "head down," "through the ball," and so on) that serve to destroy the mind-body connection required to hit a good shot.

"A swing takes .9 to 1.1 seconds—and so many things happen," Yoni says. "We should have only—at most—one thing on our minds when standing over the ball, yet technical instruction is based on memorizing facts, details, and approaches. People stand over the ball with their mind racing; your brain and central nervous system feel and react to this. It creates tension in the body."

And all of that is very bad. Yoni and I have lived this. We have taken the lessons and become overloaded with anywhere from two to twenty thoughts in our minds while addressing the ball. It's no way to play, nor is it any way to go through life. It's the definition of "being in your head," which is where I live—and a dark place from which I would like to flee. But Yoni is going to teach me that being there is okay, so long as we are there in a good way.

o o o o

After twenty-five minutes we arrive in the parking lot of Yoni's nondescript brown high-rise apartment building, which is surrounded by numerous other identical nondescript brown high-rise apartment buildings. This is not what I'd expected. Yes, it's winter, but I was anticipating an indoor driving range or a renovated loft somewhere downtown. A chill runs down my spine as we walk, and I am overcome by the realization that I am with someone I met on the Internet.

Thus, as we enter the building and go downstairs where Yoni opens the basement door, I am relieved to find a makeshift one-stall driving range that consists of an Astroturf mat and a large net, rather than a soundproof torture chamber where I will be ritually slaughtered with a 6-iron. By the time Yoni hands me my putter, my fight-or-flight mechanism has returned my inner state to a low, anxious hum.

That we begin with putting is strange, as it is a stroke so personal, so idiosyncratic, that I've always thought it was nearly impossible to teach. But Yoni says that it is a small, quiet movement in which he can begin to see and assess rhythms and little things that will only be magnified as we take full swings with the other clubs in my bag.

I putt ten balls. All of them travel roughly the same distance and come to rest not far from each other. Yoni asks me to putt ten more with my eyes closed. I am to concentrate on my rhythm and awareness of where in my body I feel the shot. Then he says to move my awareness around—to my hands, my arms, my shoulders, and finally my pelvis. This stop on the tour of my body makes the stroke feel so uncoordinated and nonrhythmic that I am reminded of why I don't dance—ever.

When we get to my feet, Yoni explains that they—somewhat obviously—represent my connection to the earth. I pay attention to where I am balancing my weight. Quickly I realize that it is mostly in my heels—and I know this is bad. Yoni, however, won't go there. He gives me a pleasant look that says, "Don't judge. Just be aware."

I do my best, but I am still trapped in the Western quick-fix-oriented mindset. Thus, I wait about ten seconds and ask Yoni what's up with my swing. What has my putting taught him?

Yoni is reluctant—and I respect that. He tells me that, ordinarily, he takes time with his analysis and always keeps in mind that his instant judgment may well be wrong. It's a good philosophy and in keeping with the open-minded, learning-based ideas behind Feldenkrais. But I press him and, since we only have four or five hours together, he makes an exception.

My swing, he thinks, might—just might—rely a bit too heavily on my arms and hands. This does two things: 1) it probably makes me swing too fast and 2) it causes me to use more effort than I would if I were engaging my hips, shoulders, and torso more fully. The second part is the key to getting more power with less effort. And believe me, I haven't lost sight of that goal.

Getting to effortless, however, might not be as easy as I'd hoped. Earlier Yoni had told me something to the effect of "Give me a beginner and I'll make a golfer. Give me a golfer, well, that's a more difficult task."

This is a variation on the classic Buddhist concept of "Beginner's Mind," which advocates openness of mind and avoidance of preconceptions. In fact, it's a very nice turn on Shunryu Suzuki's famous quote, "In the beginner's mind there are many possibilities. In the expert's mind there are few."

And I, despite my better intentions, probably fall into the latter category. Feldenkrais, much to its credit, is rooted in the former.

The method was the brainchild of Moshe Feldenkrais, who in 1946—at the age of forty-two—re-aggravated an old knee injury. An accomplished engineer and a judo black belt, he declined surgery and developed his own method of rehab based on body awareness techniques that straddle—but are not limited to—several disciplines: yoga, massage, tai chi, Reiki, and meditation breathwork. Synthesizing these into a single technique that involved small, nonstrenuous movements that encourage increased awareness of your physical limitations, Feldenkrais healed himself. Then, during the next several decades, the charismatic, gruff, and egotistical creator of this method set out to heal the world, teaching across the United States and Europe. And though it is hardly as well known as yoga or Pilates, google Feldenkrais practitioners in your city and you will probably find several.

Feldenkrais himself believed that our physical limitations have a great deal to do with the limitations of our mind, believing that a flexible brain could help "make the impossible possible, the possible easy, and the easy elegant." And he used the method to great effect on everyone from the badly injured to children with cerebral palsy, and to people like me, who simply want to improve their functioning in a specific area.

The bottom line of his philosophy was: "Find your true weakness and surrender to it. Therein lies the path to genius."

As Yoni and I stand there, I attempt to surrender to my true weakness, but am too addled to locate it. Then I try to engage beginner's mind, which quickly succumbs to the more familiar thought, "Just give me a fucking club and let me show you how well I can hit the ball!!!" Which I keep to myself.

For the next forty minutes, I hit chips, pitches, and full wedge shots into a net. I can't get the feel right, nor can I gauge where the ball will go. There is something clean about each strike, but I also know that I'm not hitting it the way I should. No matter how hard I try, I simply can't slow down.

When I am done, Yoni and I discuss a few things that I ought to be "aware of." First, there are my feet—which seem to be providing not such a good connection to the earth. I swing from the heels, which I already knew. But the lack of grounding also causes a subtle hop at the back of my swing and then again when I follow through. Then it gets worse.

Yoni asks me to see how long I can hold my follow-through, and with that instruction I make a lunging swing, step in the bucket, and nearly fall over backwards. I swing again, this time more slowly, but I can't hold my pose. We do a post-mortem, and my feet look like Reggie Jackson's after a whiff.

Then Yoni briefly demonstrates the balance of his swing, which I'm not supposed to imitate or interpret as inherently correct. I can say only this: he swings twice with an absolute economy of motion that evokes images of flowing water.

When Yoni asks me to swing again, aware of my feet, it gets worse. My weight is not only in my heels, but also on the outside edges. I decide to see what happens when I move the weight .

toward my arches—which is awkward, but brings me back to the world of acceptable golf movement.

Once the footwork is better, Yoni hands me his 6-iron—my best club. The one I hit to get my game back on track when things seem to be falling apart. A few moments before, Yoni had explained how my iffy connection to the earth resulted in inadequate grounding, thus leading to tension in my feet that would creep up the body and then down my arms, creating, well, creating exactly the kind of shit-ass shots I've been hitting into the net all morning.

To get rid of this tension, Yoni says, we must use our brain. This is where it's good to be in your head, because it's the brain that knows how to balance us. When we slip on ice, it is the brain that takes over and protects us from a shattered tailbone by restoring our equilibrium.

So, my brain is supposed to balance me, but at the moment, it is occupied with more mundane thoughts like "These aren't my fucking clubs!!!" and "I haven't hit a ball in three months!!!"

Meanwhile, my discomfort is no longer just physical. I'm completely in my head, no matter how positive an experience that can potentially be. As I stew in this silent emotional maelstrom, Yoni tells me, "If we have bad static balance we can't achieve dynamic balance." I try to take this in.

This brings us into a discussion of a low-handicap, blind Israeli golfer who is one of Yoni's students. Working with the man taught Yoni a great deal. Previously, he'd believed the dictum of keeping your eye on the ball, believing that the head served a dual purpose—maintaining balance while not losing a visual focus on the point of impact.

"Our eyes are so dominant," Yoni tells me with evangelical zeal, "but [that experience] flipped it for me forever. He doesn't need to see the ball to hit it precisely. The head is for balance."

Well, whatever the hell my head is doing, it doesn't change the fact that my swing isn't fully utilizing my shoulders, torso, or pelvis. Yoni asks me to feel shots in each of those body parts and, while I can identify a thing or two (including crippling pain in my surgically repaired left knee that apparently doesn't bend that way), my primary feelings are rage and sorrow—bordering on tears.

I'm not connected to the ground. I'm swinging with my arms. I have no rhythm. Swing-wise, my pelvis is a disaster I can't even discuss. The tension Yoni spoke of has risen from my feet, down my arms, and seems likely to invade the laundry room next door.

Earlier Yoni told me that he "advocated feeling and freedom of movement," both of which sounded great. We have discussed awareness and balance to horrifying effect, without even getting much into rhythm and coordination, and nowhere near the fabled top of the FeldenGolf food chain—visualization and imagination. I remain stuck at the first level. For the next forty-five minutes I try in vain to move things in a positive direction—then I beg for help.

o o o o

There is only an hour left. I'd gotten up this morning an 18-handicapper with what I considered a nice swing, or at least that's what the pro at my local course told me one day—astonished that I wasn't in the single digits. But if something doesn't happen quickly, I will leave with a deconstructed game and no idea how to reclaim any level of proficiency or function. Which brings us to the Feldenkrais.

Yoni instructs me to lie down on the Astroturf. We are about to "connect [my] arms and hands to my shoulders and torso." So far we've been separating body parts, which I tried to rationalize as part of the "discovery process." But, silently, I am suffering cold sweats centered around flying home with a single thought: "I am going to quit this godforsaken game."

With my feet firmly on the ground, I bend my knees and put my hands together in prayer position. For the next thirty minutes I will rock back and forth with my eyes open and closed, using my shoulders (not my arms) to generate the movement. I make pretend figure-eights on the ceiling. I rock my arms in one direction and my head in the other, coordinating the two metronomes that pass each other only at twelve. I feel like a jackass, but I also become calm. Perhaps because I'm no longer swinging a club, but also because it's possible that I'm connecting with my body, a modicum of inner peace has been created.

Now, I've seen a Feldenkrais practitioner in Chicago several times. Thus I know that this is where its effects begin to resemble a bar trick or a subtle version of the eighty-year-old who does splits under hypnosis. So, I'm not surprised when, toward the end of these exercises, my arms have about 15 to 25 degrees more range of motion, which was achieved through nothing more than becoming aware of my body and how it moves.

When it is time to stand up, I feel looser. The tension has subsided a bit. The golf swing, Yoni has told me, is an "unnatural act." What he's attempted to do is to help me learn to make my body and mind adapt naturally to this unnatural act.

Before we are done, he gives me the putter again. I stroke ten balls. Though I give it some thought, my feet are balanced in the middle and towards the arches. My shoulders are now involved in the swing and generating more of the movement. When I close my eyes and try to feel the shot, I feel it everywhere and nowhere.

At no point has Yoni told me what I need to feel. Instead, he's told me to be aware and to adapt. Though his nonjudgmental direction has essentially destroyed my swing and filled me with unspoken angst, I am now focused and relaxed. These putts are the first shots that have felt good all day. And Yoni knows it.

"The pleasure is to feel that there is no effort, everything is moving together in rhythm," he says between putts. Then I hit my last. "See that? That was beauty! A yip or two, but that was beauty, right?"

A bit giddy with a mixture of awareness, newfound freedom of movement, and a huge dose of relief, I find myself agreeing.

Blue Fairways

*Skinned_Rainbow: Have you ever not created a
character for fear that it would be too terrifying?
David Lynch: Yes.
VinegarBowl: What kind of golf clubs do you use
and do you have a favorite course?
David Lynch: I am a frustrated golfer.
Irons: I use the clubs Greg Norman sells, and I use Callaway woods.*

—Excerpt from an MSN online chat with David Lynch in 2001

SPRING/SUMMER 2007. FAIRFIELD, IOWA

I came across Steve Yellin by happenstance. If I believed the idea
that there are no accidents, I'd say it was no accident.

I'd sent an email to *Blue Velvet* director David Lynch, who
had recently written a terrific meditation book entitled *Catching
the Big Fish*. On a whim I googled David Lynch and golf—and
discovered that a) he does play golf and b) it is one of the few
things he likes to watch on television.

My email, however, did not go directly to Lynch, stopping
first—and permanently—in Steve Yellin's inbox. Yellin is director

of media relations at Maharishi University in Fairfield, Iowa. Seriously. Yellin also does PR for a variety of other Transcendental Meditation organizations, hence his connection with Lynch.

Yellin's response was that we ought to talk, as he was involved with teaching nontraditional sports performance lessons that were neither "mood making" nor New Age tomfoolery.

"I'm a motion expert," he told me.

Yellin also mentioned that he is a business partner of Buddy Biancalana. Now, I'd expected that this exploration of sports, spirituality, and somewhat esoteric methods of improving one's game and life would take me down many a strange and wonderful path. Yet never, even for a second, did I suspect it would lead me to a scrappy former Kansas City Royals shortstop whose name was mentioned nearly every evening on Letterman during what seemed like all of 1985.

But, it turns out, Biancalana and Yellin had two things in common: a) both meditate and b) each has also had the profound experience of being "in the zone," for an unexpected and prolonged period of time. For Biancalana that was the 1985 World Series, during which he hit well above his career .205 average and played flawless shortstop. He was "in the zone" for the entire series, but subsequently couldn't find his way back and was out of the majors for good within eighteen months.

Nobody exactly knows who coined the term "in the zone." Yellin thinks it might have been Arthur Ashe. I just keep hearing Brent Musburger's voice repeating it over and over in my head. But "the zone" is essentially a subset of the concept of "flow," which has been the life's work of Mihaly Csikszentmihalyi, a professor at the University of Chicago who is credited with introducing it to Western psychology.

"In the zone" has been defined as becoming completely absorbed in whatever you are doing, to the extent that your actions and awareness merge, bringing great satisfaction, pleasure, and contentment—as well as what is usually near-optimal performance. The idea of flow or the zone, however, wasn't created in the last thirty years. It is in many ways rooted in Buddhism and Taoism. It is "being the ball" in whatever you do. Pelé described it this way:

"I felt a strange calmness . . . a kind of euphoria. I felt I could run all day without tiring, that I could dribble through any of their team or all of them, that I could almost pass through them physically."

Csikszentmihalyi believes it is those moments "in the zone" that give meaning to our otherwise shitty lives. Most people, he says, live at one of two extremes—either anxiety or boredom. Those times where we are in the flow "provide the flashes of intense living against this dull background."

Yikes. But maybe true. And maybe even truer as we age.

Yellin's experience was in February of 1975, while he was the #1 singles player on the University of Pennsylvania tennis team. Burned out after a lifetime of competition, he played a match where suddenly everything was effortless, effective, and seamless. He was "in the zone" the entire match.

"That one experience led to everything that I've done since," he told me.

Here's what went down. For years, much as he loved tennis, Yellin played to win. He played for ego. He had almost no interest or even understanding of "the deep inner satisfaction of the process of playing a match." Like most of us, he was motivated by results.

By his senior year at Penn, Yellin had been All-Ivy a few times, but was mentally exhausted and felt as if he was just going through the motions on the court. Then, while playing a match against an opponent he'd beaten before, Yellin noticed something subtle—but distinct and profound—during warm-ups.

"It was like one of those experiences you read about in books, but it's happening to you," he told me. "It was as if a blanket of peace and silence was thrown over me."

At first he was stunned, even thrown a bit. The court, which had always been a battlefield, was suddenly a magical place where he was playing, rather than competing. His priorities were different. The experience of hitting the ball became ultimately satisfying. It was all that intrigued him. Winning became not only secondary; it became tertiary, subterranean—even nonexistent. Yellin no longer cared about the other side of the court. All that mattered was his experience, which was "mental, physical, even spiritual."

With that he began to play "out of his mind." There was a sense that his body was doing things without the use of his brain—he was almost witnessing his own actions, which were suddenly fluid and effortless. It was as if he'd been taken over by a "higher creative power."

When the match was over, Yellin didn't feel mentally or physically drained. Instead, he'd drawn even greater energy from the experience. A religion major, he'd long wanted to understand life in a more profound way. And for those few hours he'd found peace, silence, and a deeper aspect of reality.

"It was not only the most profound experience I've had in tennis, but also in my life," he said.

Here was the problem. After thinking about it for a few days, Yellin found that he couldn't repeat it. Being "in the zone" had appeared magically and disappeared just as quickly. He thought about it for an entire year, hoping to unlock the mechanics of that transformational experience. With time, he came to understand that being "in the zone" wasn't about what you were doing physically. It was about what you were doing when you weren't moving. When you weren't hitting the ball. Everything happened "in the gap," during moments of inaction.

"What I'd experienced when I was doing nothing was infinitely more important than what I'd experienced when I was acting," he told me on the phone. "I had this deep feeling that I could teach this. Not some mystical, out-of-the-ordinary psychic experience that comes of its own volition. The essential ingredient of the experience was the inaction."

Okay, I was intrigued. Improving things by improving the quality of the moments when I wasn't doing anything—a field in which I'm an eminent scholar—this was a step beyond effortless.

Yellin then described how he'd unlocked the key to creating conditions by which an athlete could put himself "in the zone" at will. Maybe not completely, but at least help it happen on a more regular basis.

It all had to do with the gap and how inaction created the action. Yellin told me it worked like this. If you went to the U.S. Open tennis tournament and watched warm-ups, it'd be hard to discern the difference between the #25 and #250 players in the world. All of them have beautiful serves and groundstrokes. It seems almost inconceivable that any of them can lose. And he's right. The same applies to swings on the range before a tournament, where the worst guy out there laid several supremely difficult courses to waste with 63s fired at Q-School or on the Hooters Tour. Yet, when the game starts, something else happens.

It's not pressure, according to Yellin. Pressure—for most good athletes—he says, is a variable that can be isolated and controlled. Yes, there is the odd choke artist (see: anyone who has every worn a Chicago Cubs uniform; and Greg Norman), but over time nearly all of these guys have dealt with enough pressure that they can handle it.

Instead, Yellin told me, when the games start, you can notice something that is quite subtle, but that we've all seen or experienced. The difference between the #25 and #250 tennis players is this: When their opponent hits a serve that is a quarter of an inch out, #250 often hits a blazing backhand return down the line and that lands just in at the far corner; the same player, however, faced with a similar serve that is a quarter of an inch in will make a pedestrian return. Something happens in that split second of inaction when the athlete's brain computes whether the serve is in or out that creates the motion that will be their return. A split-second decision happens in that gap of inaction. And that is what determines the quality of the shot.

I recently read that the actual "playing" of a round of golf—the time we are hitting the ball or putting—occurs in roughly 180 seconds within the four hours we are on the course. What's happening the rest of the time, where our mind resides during that time, is something we pay almost no attention to, yet which profoundly impacts our performance.

While his theory of inaction "in the gap" as the determining force of all action was evolving, Yellin tried it out as a tennis instructor, eventually hooking up with Biancalana and forming "Perfect Mind, Perfect Motion," whose students range from college golf and tennis teams to former baseball phenoms who are struggling to "find it" again in the minors. The entire focus is on how to create effortless action via what we do when we're not moving. It is about understanding motion at its most fundamental level—where it originates.

During our long phone conversation we also covered a bit of Vedic philosophy, string theory, and unified field theory—all of which came up in varying degrees,[1] but which Yellin didn't want to emphasize. He invited me to Fairfield, where he'd show me drills that allow athletes to put themselves "in the zone" or at least create the conditions most favorable to entry. I nearly jumped through the phone.

Soon I'd convinced myself that somehow—very quickly—I was going to be able to put myself "in the zone" at will. During the ten days that separated our conversation and my trip to Iowa, I began to warn my regular golf partners that they ought to play with me now. Right now. Because soon, I would be "in the zone" 24/7, perhaps only coming out of the zone to remember what it was like to not be "in the zone"—just for the challenge.

---

1 He is not alone. *Golf in the Kingdom* is peppered with references to various aspects of quantum physics, while Kjell Enhager's *Quantum Golf* includes the following as applied to the game:

Instructor: "It has to do with the particle and the field . . . in quantum physics, the particle is no longer solid. It's just a bump or wave in the field. The field is the primary reality; it's everything and everywhere, an infinite field underlying all diversity."
Student: "An infinite what?"
Instructor: "An unbounded, unmanifest, and perfectly ordered unified state. A unified field connecting everything."
Student: "What does this all this have to do with . . . my golf swing?"
Instructor: "Everything."

Then I would re-enter the zone again, because that's where I intended to take up permanent residence.

I began to consider what it might be like to live "in the zone" both personally and on the course. How I'd lose all of my anxieties and inhibitions. How trips to the grocery store and the removal of dog vomit from our living room rug would become sublime moments of deep fulfillment. What's not to like about always being "in the zone"? Can I sleep "in the zone"? Will I die if I'm always "in the zone," or will I be able to cure the cancer when it finally comes knocking?

Then I started to worry. I wondered if I was seeing Yellin too early in the process and wouldn't need further instruction, rendering the journey in this book useless after Chapter 3. I countered this by reasoning that I'd also be writing in the zone, so it'd probably be a masterpiece no matter what happened. Yet, my apprehensions got the better of me and I decided to forgo listening to subliminal meditation and relaxation tapes on the drive from Chicago to Fairfield for fear of prematurely gilding the metaphysical Buddhist golfing lily.

o o o o

Maharishi University sits on 250 acres that Maharishi Mahesh Yogi himself bought in 1974 after its previous occupant—Parsons College—went belly up. Having once learned a bit about the fourteen-year-old Perfect Master who had acquired large portions of Malibu in the early 70s, I've begun to realize that for some gurus, enlightenment often brings with it shrewd judgment regarding real estate.

Arriving in town, I call Yellin and he tells me to continue driving down B Street and I'd see him in about a mile. I do so and after three minutes I spot a tall man in a yellow golf shirt, elastic-waist khakis, sandals, and a baseball hat standing by the side of the road.

"You Steve?" I call out.

He makes some kind of welcoming gesture and walks towards a decrepit Victorian home. I pull into the driveway and he walks towards me.

"Sorry, I almost missed you," I say.

"Sure. No problem," he says. Up close he is a soft, slouchy, John Malkovich type with a grey goatee.

"Well, great to meet you," I say, holding out my hand, only to find him pulling out the waistband of his pants and readjusting his shirt.

"Yeah, you too."

"Where are we going?" I ask.

"Who are you again?" he asks without malice.

"I'm Josh Karp. The writer. We talked a few minutes ago. Are you Steve?"

"Steve who?"

"Steve Yellin."

"No, I'm not even named Steve. So, you're a writer?"

"Yeah?"

"What are you writing about?"

"I'm doing a golf book."

"Then Steve Yellin is your guy."

"You know him?"

"No, but I know Jerry Yellin. Ask Steve to tell you about Jerry and his wife. That'd make a good story for what you're writing."

"I'll do that," I say, trying to begin a graceful exit. He continues, "Turns out Jerry married a Japanese gal and her dad was a Kamikaze pilot in the War." [2]

Though harmless, he is giving off a subtle *Silence of the Lambs* vibe.

"Uh-huh," I say cautiously, as I beep my car door, hoping to signal imminent departure.

"Well, Jerry's dad was a fighter pilot in the Pacific," he says, unfazed. "And they had to go to Japan to meet her folks."

"Wow, I gotta run because . . ."

"So, do you write screenplays?"

"No. Wish I did," I say, hopping into my car. "Great meeting you."

He waves goodbye and I beep as I make it back onto B Street, where in three blocks—at the intersection of B and Taste of Utopia—I see a man in an orange golf shirt and a beaming smile, who turns out to be Steve Yellin.

He was fifty-four years old—the same age as Yoni—a bit under 5′10″, trim and athletic in that former tennis prodigy way. I'd have been hard pressed to pinpoint his age: He could have been forty-four or a well-preserved fifty-nine. Yellin takes me to lunch at the school's cafeteria, which is noted for wonderful

---

2 Almost a year later, Yellin included me in a mass email promoting his father Jerry's book *The Blackened Canteen*—which led me to JerryYellin.com and the revelation that one of Yellin's brothers indeed did marry a Japanese woman and Yellin's father did serve in World War II, bringing about some version of the story told above, which is chronicled in Jerry's *Of War and Weddings*.

vegetarian fare and—by me—for a unique level of hygiene I can only describe as dusty.

Yellin is a man of great and genuine enthusiasm. When he gets into my Toyota Prius he says, "You're gonna love it here. You're in the Prius capital of the world. Everybody here has a Prius." His vibrancy is infectious; I decline to share that one of the worst things about driving a Prius is the "community" of fellow drivers with their "Eat My Voltage" bumper stickers and the "I'm listening to *All Things Considered* but I'm taking a moment to give you a thumbs up for joining me in saving the planet" looks I get on a daily basis.

After lunch we head to Dick's Long Shot Driving Range, which is literally cut out of the middle of an Iowa cornfield with a few rubber mats and about a 300-yard poke to where the maize starts.

We briefly go over some of what we'd already discussed: the inaction, the gap, the creation of motion in moments of non-motion. Yellin gives me a few drills on which I'm sworn to secrecy. But, here is the best way I can describe what I learned during our ninety-minute session.

There are three conditions that must be created for one to get "in the zone."

Time Moves Normally. This might seem obvious. But it's not distorted the way you hear Gretzky, Magic, or Bird describing how everyone else seems to be moving in slow motion when they play. More likely, they are experiencing things as they actually unfold—in real time. Others, who aren't in the zone, are experiencing the distortion. For instance, it's safe to assume that when any Detroit Lions quarterback drops back to pass, the field before him probably looks like an army of ants in different colored jerseys running around a hill as if on fast forward. It's safe to assume that this is not what Tom Brady sees. He experiences the few seconds between the snap and hitting his receiver deep down the sideline in . . . exactly a few seconds.

Your Intellect Shuts Down. This is easy to understand. It's the thing we've all experienced on some level, whether at work, hanging with your kids, or playing basketball in the driveway with everything you toss going in. You're not thinking. Everything just happens and you instinctively know what to do—and .when you don't know what to do, you don't sweat it or observe it very much. Instead you just keep going, without thought. It's being in the flow.

When the two prior conditions exist, the optimal result is that you activate your fast-twitch muscles at a far higher level than usual. This is where the motion becomes sublime and effortless rather than conscious and labored. This is where you catch the ball, turn and hit only net from 25 feet. It is where you feel the guy rushing from behind during the Thanksgiving Day football game. It is what happens when your imperfect golf swing corrects itself over and over again during the course of a round without your thinking, "tempo, tempo, tempo." Your intuition is firing on all cylinders and controlling your body and its actions.

To paraphrase Shivas Irons, you are neither trying too hard nor thinking too much.

After some warm-ups, Yellin explains that we don't ultimately have control over our motion. We can only control where the motion originates.

"It's like looking at a tree," he tells me. "You don't have control over the branches and leaves, but you do have it over the roots."

We discussed Tiger and Roger Federer and how they describe some of their actions—moments we can assume they were "in the zone." Tiger once said that he'd hit a great shot and didn't even remember taking his club out of the bag or swinging. Federer, the same, saying that he's at his best when he doesn't "know that he's in a point." Perhaps this is why Jordan shrugged to Magic during his insane three-point barrage against Portland in the 1992 NBA Finals. Maybe he was simply acknowledging that he had no idea what he was doing, but the ball just kept going in.

How do they get there? They don't think about the result, according to Yellin. The result is what he calls your "DNA Goal." It's concrete. And the essence of his method is focusing your mind on something abstract, so as to almost distract yourself from that concrete DNA goal and to get yourself into "the zone."

Tiger, Jordan, Federer, and their peers "become abstract when others become concrete."

Now, you can't just tell yourself to not think or to become abstract. You can't tell time to move normally. You can't say, "Be smooth, effortless, and powerful," and then just make that happen. That's just more thinking.

So we get into the drills that will help me "sink deeper into the field of abstraction." This will free my mind, ultimately taking it off the shot and placing it on something intangible—thus creating the motion from a place of freedom, rather than from a world of results and swing thoughts. Yellin is smiling. He is nearly beatific standing there on the next rubber mat. I am a bit dubious.

Handing me my 6-iron, Yellin has me focus on one thing: how I feel standing over the ball. As I hit ball after ball, I become more aware of this "feeling" rather than the action of the swing. My goal is to get as comfortable as possible and to know what that feels like and to do it every time. It's not easy. I think about the swing a lot. "That's not only a waste of time—" he says, "it's a destructive waste of time." But, I think about my swing. A lot. Then, with a bit of practice I get myself about 60 percent there.

It's a fairly radical approach. If you don't believe me, pick up a copy of *Golf Digest* and look at the dozens of articles telling you how to stand, where to stand, where your divot ought to be, and things I can't even begin to understand on the page, let alone incorporate into my game. Yellin's approach disregards all of that, basically giving over to the fact that my swing, while technically imperfect, is good enough. I am supposed to give up, not think, and simply create the freedom within my mind and body to be fluid, which will allow my body to adjust and maximize my capacity to hit the ball.

After moderately getting a handle on finding a comfortable setup, Yellin asks me to focus on how I feel after the shot. I am to get equally comfortable on the other side of my shot. When that is integrated, I am to combine the two, concentrating on the two bookends of inaction—setup and finish—and nothing else. At one point, I feel a warmth in the center of my chest that is nothing like a heart attack. Unexpectedly, it is something like peace. It is brief and it happens in a cornfield driving range not far from Taste of Utopia Street, all of which make me immediately suspicious. And like my other experiences with such peace, it disappears the second I recognize it.

With some difficulty I am able to drop down into the field of abstraction more and more. Before we leave, I pick up my old

Cobra driver with the offset head. I follow the protocol and, for the first time in twenty years, hit the ball 260 yards and straight.

That is it. Yellin smiles broadly. He tells me to try to focus on those simple lessons and we are done. Nothing, I think, can be this simple.

o o o o

Three days later I headed out to Glencoe Golf Club and hit about twenty-five practice balls with my 7-iron before a noon tee time. With each shot I sought to get abstract. And each shot was more horrific than the last. I was so loose and focused else-where that I was barely getting my 7-iron in the air. But on the tee, I stayed with the plan and did what Yellin had taught me.

I doubled the first, as I almost always do. But, I didn't sweat it. I let go of the results in my swing and on my scorecard. Which was good, as I tripled two.

On the third, a short par-4, I hit my 3-iron far right and into the trees off the tee—from where I was playing it safe. I punched out and hit a short pitch onto the green to about 15 feet left of the cup. Not an impressive shot in the bunch. On the green, I looked at the hole, lined myself up, and forgot all about what I was doing. Instead, I focused on being comfortable before and after the shot. I focused on it feeling good and nothing else. I ran the ball right into the center of the hole as if I did it all the time. Likewise, on four, a sand save to within inches saved par again. I was with the program.

After a huge drive and 7-iron approach to within 15 feet on five, I two-putted for par. Another big drive on six had me thinking about finishing the rest of the front in even par and shooting a 41. I capitalized on that drive by hitting three consecutive 5-to-15 foot duffs and took a triple. I then went bogey, par, par to finish with a 45 on the front.

On the tenth, a 425-yard par-4, I hit a lousy drive in the long rough on the right, probably about 210 yards from the tee. I couldn't see the green; I had no club that goes 215 out of the rough, so I picked up my 6-iron, figuring I'd hit a nice shot out to the fairway and get on in 3. Then I stopped. I pulled out my 5-wood, which I hadn't hit in three years but still kept in my bag. I took a few practice swings, got a decent idea of the direction in which I wanted to go, and hit away.

I knew that I'd struck it pretty well and figured I'd be in the fairway 30 yards short. But even as I got closer I couldn't see my ball. I looked everywhere in front and—trying to be inconspicuous—walked on the green and glanced in the hole. It wasn't there. Instead, it was 10 feet off the back. I'd hit a 220ish-yard 5-wood. It was better than having holed out. I chipped up and drained my putt for par.

The rest of the back was like some kind of dream. I bogeyed four holes and parred everything else. On a dogleg right, I swung away without a thought in my head and watched my drive turn at the 230-yard bend and go 30 yards further to the center of the fairway. When I needed to make the ball go straight, that happened too. I shot a 40, my lowest score for nine holes in at least a decade. While I wasn't "in the zone" the entire time, I was having zone-like results and was totally free of tension, having a blast, and as completely present as I'd ever been on a golf course. It wasn't transcendent. But it was effortless, and my best score so far this year—85 with two triples.

I called Yellin. For the only time in my entire life I was telling a proud teacher about our mutual success.

"You crossed over 180 degrees from understanding it as a series of motions to a series of inactions, which is the most important thing," he said. "It took you out of prison. You were liberated from your mental prison."

He may have been happier than I was. Perhaps I had "the secret," I thought. I called my father and told him what I'd learned. He went out the next day and shot a "good 89" after weeks of not having played. I began to feel as if I'd had some kind of ecstatic golfing vision and was judiciously sending its message to a select few. I was soon to be on my way to Portland to see Jim Waldron at the Balance Point Golf School. And though I was pretty sure I didn't need his help, I figured I'd teach him a thing or two about how to get your mind right.

Lost in the Maze

*Golf is a game that is played on a five-inch
course—the distance between your ears.*

–BOBBY JONES

It's nice, this idea of the authentic swing. Though rooted in a
Hindu tale, it's essentially the Buddhist belief that if we can clear
away all of our protection and neurotic crap, we are all perfect.
That letting go will reveal our inner magnificence. It's a rich
and comforting concept—within us is a magical, happy person
who can play scratch golf. Life and golf are intertwined journeys
toward a nirvana that is in our heart.

I love it, frankly. It means that I'm okay and you're okay.
Though it shouldn't be confused with the book *I'm OK, You're
OK*, which your neo-feminist college girlfriend tried to get you
to read sophomore year. No, it's that you are fine as you are and
that all you really need to do is find yourself. And really, how
hard can it be to find yourself, as night after night you are right
there, lying on the sofa watching *Law & Order SVU* reruns on

USA after the kids are in bed. In whatever case, if you succeed in this endeavor, the riches of human existence and a cure to your duck hook await.

I love this "less is more" kind of thinking. The idea that relaxing is the key to locating the real me. I've found, however, that this "finding myself" business is as difficult as explaining why I watched *The Pope of Greenwich Village* hundreds of times between the ages of nineteen and twenty-three.

In the wake of my lesson from Steve Yellin and its glorious aftermath, I believed that I was about to find my authentic swing. A trip out to Oregon and Jim Waldron's Balance Point Golf School, I thought, would provide a few cosmic swing changes, and I'd be on my way to becoming the suburban, "Juddhist" Jack Nicklaus. I assumed that I was not far from total integration as a man and a golfer.

I was soon disabused of this notion.

On a cool, dewy morning I meet Waldron on the practice tee at Quail Valley Golf Club in Banks, Oregon, about ninety minutes outside of Portland. Behind a pair of reflective aviator shades and under a floppy hat was a man whose curly, graying hair and tie-dyed handkerchief evoked a bit of Donald Sutherland.

That morning on the range, I may have swung the club six or seven times. I intended to, and he certainly wanted to see what my game was all about. But instead, I spent the better part of four hours writing. Furiously. A self-described polymath, Waldron worked like a jazz musician, rattling off and explaining a variety of influences, concepts, gurus, and other golf/life-related ephemera. A woefully incomplete list of things that came up during a day and a half on that tee would include the Alexander Technique and the Stanislavski Method; karate and kung fu; Dr. Bob Rotella and the fact that no one is ever "aware" when they are in the midst of a head-on collision; Gestalt therapy and the body-mind connection; 9/11 and the space shuttle; Ben Hogan and Bones McCoy; Abraham Maslow, the father of humanist psychology, and Mac O'Grady, golf's foremost swing theorist; the Neolithic period and John Wooden—an apropos tandem; sensory channels and the night sky; Noam Chomsky and flotation tanks. I am only scratching the surface. Most of all, however, his thoughts on the authentic swing remain burned in my consciousness.

"There is no swing that you were born with," he tells me, "That's a bunch of bullshit. Have you ever heard a piano teacher talking about that kind of crap? Finding your inner pianist?"

Point well taken and definitely food for thought, as I've never heard of Roger Clemens having tapped his inner dickheaded roid-monster or read reference to when Picasso found the Cubist within.

But golfers, even if they don't call it the authentic swing, have a belief that somehow, some way, they are great and that one, two, or three lessons won't just make them better. They believe that they will achieve some country club version of what the Buddhists call satori—instant enlightenment. Fifteen strokes will magically disappear and if only they'd started out younger, they could be on the tour.

Circling back to the piano analogy, Waldron likens it to someone "expecting to have a few lessons and suddenly they are Mozart."

More simply put, it is Frank Costanza screaming to the heavens, "SERENITY NOW!!! SERENITY NOW!!!"

And then we talk about rats in a maze.

The concept, he tells me, is random reinforcement. You put a bunch of rats in the maze and place food at the end. On day one, they are released into the labyrinth and take maybe forty-five minutes to reach their reward. The second day, they have learned a bit, know a few of the turns to take and get there in thirty minutes. Day three, however, is a bad one for the rats. They make their way even faster, but at the end there is no food. Not a kernel of corn, a grain of rice, or plate of Nachos Bell Grande. Nothing.

All kinds of variations can follow. Some days, the food is there. Some days it isn't. There is no rhyme or reason. Some rats are allowed to pull a lever and receive their food without making the journey. Other times they get it for scratching their face. But once they acclimate to a predictable outcome, that a certain action will bring a certain result—well, then the rug is pulled out and there is no pattern. Some rats scratch their faces until they die.

The bottom line here has several components, which are the reasons you and I should care about these rats. First, under such conditions, effective learning is impossible. Directly related to this is Waldron's belief that most of us with a handicap over 15 are not so unlike these rats.

"There is a mentally ill culture related to golf," he says. "It's based on random reinforcement and an industry driven by people who don't know they are addicts."

Let's look at it another way. Random reinforcement underlies gambling addiction, which Waldron tells me is harder to kick than heroin. The reason for this? With heroin, the more an addict uses the drug, the more he needs of it to get high. He builds up a tolerance to its effects, which are predictable. With gambling, the high never dissipates, because it is undependable and not within the addict's control. You can fail and fail and fail and then succeed on a large scale. Its random nature only serves to reinforce the gambler's belief that they did something right that brought about a positive result, when in reality most gambling addicts have the same impact on their success as a Native American rain dance has on precipitation.

"When you expect success at a difficult task and achieve it 80 percent of the time or better, that's a skill; 90 percent and you're a tour player. But otherwise it's random," Waldron tells me. "Occasionally you'll hit a good shot. It sounds louder. It feels more solid. Your brain produces neurochemicals. It secretes serotonin and hormones that make you feel good. It secretes beta-endorphins, norepinephrine, and dopamine. You are more excited about your infrequent successes than your frequent failures."

Thus, that sudden string of pars or straight 270-yard drives are a big part of the problem. They are our rain dance. Our trip through the maze.

"You pull the lever for more cocaine," he says. "When we get lucky, we get happy about the fact that we got lucky and it's imprinted on our subconscious. Everybody remembers where they were on 9/11. That's because of the emotional impact."

To follow that analogy, the higher your handicap, the more you are like Rudy Giuliani post-2001. Before it's all over, you are convinced that you personally pulled hundreds of doomed individuals out of harm's way before catching Osama Bin Laden and killing him with your bare hands. Or, maybe it's your belief that the tip from *Golf Digest*, the one where you pretend a ball in the sand is a Danish, helped you break 90 twice last weekend and is the missing link between you and consistent mid-80s golf.

Waldron thinks all of this is actually the placebo effect, and that golfers begin believing their own guesses. It works for a while, and then you go back to the same hack you were two weeks before.

"It's golf-swing metaphysics. People start making up shit about why they hit the ball better," he says. "It's golf in the Bizarro World. It's not golf. It's flog."

And then we break for lunch, where I learn a few things about Waldron. He is a native Chicagoan and a baby boomer; he went to New College and was beaten up at the 1968 Democratic Convention. At a young age he took up martial arts after reading the classic *Zen Flesh, Zen Bones* and studied with a Zen monk with high-degree black belts in karate and judo. Give the monk a degree in philosophy from NYU, and he's Patrick Swayze in *Roadhouse.*

Waldron took up golf at ten. Soon thereafter he shot an 80. When he was fifteen, he shot a 68 on the first day of a tournament. Then, after shooting an 82 in the second round, he put down his clubs for eleven years, at which point he hit a few balls at Tilden Park in Berkeley and realized that he was as good as he'd ever been. After a few weeks, he was actually much better. The absence of traditional instruction had done nothing but help him. In the back of his mind, Waldron decided that one day he'd make golf his career.

In between that fateful day and 1995, Waldron did many things. He did some odd jobs, a bit of plumbing and construction. During the 1980s oil recession he was involved in an alternative energy venture. Later he indulged his passion for scuba diving with an excursion business. His priorities were clear.

"Money was always at the bottom of my list," he tells me. "I was always more interested in learning stuff. How I could obtain enlightenment."

In this way he was like Billy Crystal in City Slickers, who learned to follow his bliss. Though, in truth, Waldron is far deeper than any bit of armchair philosophy one might glean from a movie written by Lowell Ganz and Babaloo Mandel.

Along the way, he floated in a sensory-deprivation tank, exploring the workings of his mind; studied Neurolinguistic Programming (NLP) and learned how to delete unwanted behaviors; and deconstructed the golf swing with Mac O' Grady. In 1995, he fused it all together and started Balance Point, with a focus on the mind–body connection.

"I'd always seen it," he says of melding the brain and body. "Even when I was a kid."

This, however, doesn't mean that his is a touchy-feely, New Age enterprise. Laid back but opinionated, Waldron employs a teaching method that is old school, born of the martial arts dojo, where Sensei knows best. He doesn't seek to be worshipped or obeyed, but he also doesn't want to hear: "Are you sure that's right? I don't think so. It's really uncomfortable."

Golfers seem to ask those kinds of questions and make a lot of such statements. Rarely, I'd assume, have such questions been asked of guys like Bear Bryant and Bobby Knight. And if they had been, I imagine someone is still trying to remove a clipboard from a long-deceased sophomore point guard's head.

Waldron's philosophy is that feel, mind state, and all of that have their place. But that the golf swing is the golf swing. It is a "devilish thing," as Hogan once said, and it can be approached via nontraditional methods, but it is also science, not New Age mumbo jumbo.

"It's an objective model. It's just like the space shuttle," he says. "Nobody ever came home and said, 'I altered the laws of physics today' based on a dream or feeling."

Getting back to the rats, this is all part of the ultimate lesson. Yes, we are all mentally ill. Indeed, an idiot slapping bucket after bucket of worm-burning 8-irons is not so different from the blue-haired lady who just got off the bus from Hot Springs and plans to spend three consecutive days dropping tokens in a slot machine.

But more importantly, there is this: We should avoid scratching our faces off and instead buckle down, shut our mouths, and make the journey.

Which is what I decide I must do after one of Waldron's students, whom we'll call Chet, comes over and diagnoses the problems with my swing.

Okay, now Chet, despite being a goateed 12-handicap, is a good guy—and he's not acting alone like Lee Harvey Oswald in a pair of FootJoys. Instead, as I finally begin to hit balls—and hit them well in my estimation—Waldron asks if Chet is seeing what he is seeing.

They both saw this: 1) I have spine angle issues. Namely, I am a bit hunched over. 2) My balance could be a bit better. I am standing up a bit at the end of my swing, rather than staying down. This is because I have a tendency to do what Little League coaches call "stepping in the bucket" at the end of my swing: essentially falling backward a bit with my front foot. Good thing I'm at a place called "Balance Point," I think to myself, though I must say my inner voice had a bit of sarcasm. Finally, 3) the most painful of them all. My swing is not a long, smooth arc, as I supposed. No, I am doing what they call "coming over the top," which means that I am out of position as I begin my downswing and use whatever natural athletic ability I possess to put the club back in the proper plane. In fact, they both say some version of "It's amazing you can actually hit the ball well doing that."

I think I must be guessing right pretty often, though probably not at the 80 to 90 percent level. That this criticism is coming from a guy I might beat every once in a while—and whose facial hair will someday go the way of Rollie Fingers'— does sting a bit. In some minor way although I'm suffering what my former therapist would term either a "narcissistic injury" or a "psychic storm," I keep my cool. Some combo of having been in the zone and increased meditation tells me that it's okay. Yes, I must make the journey. Which I do when faced with the following choice: "Do you want to maximize your imperfect swing? Or do you want to create a new, better one?"

There is really only one answer, even if I'm leaving on a 5 P.M. flight out of Portland the next day.

Waldron asks me some questions about this new swing.

What color is it?

Blue.

What shape is it?

Round.

Is it still or pulsing?

Both; it depends.

Our end goal is to enhance the mind-body connection. Which is a pretty big catchall, but here's an idea of its application

to golf as interpreted by Waldron: When the mind-body connection is working properly, the brain and the body are not
only in sync, but are operating at the same speed. Think about
it. What makes for most shitty golf swings? Mostly, they occur
when a series of moving parts are not meshing properly. When
the hips turn too early on the downswing and the hands lag
behind, when we accidentally shorten our backswing and the
club comes down a tenth of a second before it is supposed to and
makes you hit it fat. You know it somewhere, if you'd stop and
think about it. You can feel it.

Therefore, we want to create a system in which there is
seamless communication of data from our brain to our muscles
and joints. We want to be alert, awake, and attentive, glued to a
focal point, but passive and relaxed. No sweat.

To do this, Waldron tells me we will seek to find the root
cause of my problems. If we figure this out, then there will be a
breakthrough—the one that happens during therapy in movies
and has not happened to anyone you have ever known.

We begin with focal points. Waldron says that there is a long
list of focal points—and there is a forbidden list. Two of the more
common you might find among the latter are being ball bound
and swing bound.

Swing bound is a "neurotic attachment." It is the constant
stream of swing thoughts, rattling off a list of fundamentals and
tricks and stuff you've been told by that guy you paired up with
a few weeks back who shot a 38 on the back. I have dispensed
such advice; God help those who received it. There are tricks
to cure this. You can count backwards from 100 by threes while
swinging. You can repeat the number "seventeen," as Waldron
tells me Vijay Singh does.

Ball bound is "a mild mental illness." It is the worst thing you can be thinking about. Yet, says Waldron, "It's pretty much what everyone thinks about when they hit the ball."

What is happening here is that we are misconstruing the ball as the target. Now, of course we are trying to hit the ball. But, like Dr. Phil's advice, the "ball as target" realm of belief makes very little sense when held up to scrutiny. Does Peyton Manning look at the ball while Marvin Harrison cuts across the middle? Okay, Rex Grossman actually does look at the ball, but he's an anomaly. Did Larry Bird look at the ball? Hell, half of the time he wasn't even looking at the target—and it always made its way there. Most importantly, however, have you ever seen an archer look at the bow and arrow? No, they are looking at the target. And this is where your attention should be focused as well. You want to hit the target with the ball, not the ball with the club. If you remember nothing else, remember this.

This is where Waldron took me into the four mind states. Being ball bound and swing bound are both conscious-mind activities. This dimension is responsible for active thinking, effort, will power, making choices. It is aware of itself and is able to make changes during action. The conscious mind is no place from which to play golf. It is the place of swing thoughts, neuroses, and mental illness—at least on the course.

"In the United States and Japan we try to use the conscious mind to make changes during the swing," Waldron says. "It's sheer folly and fucking insanity."

If the conscious mind is you sitting at a computer typing a letter, the subconscious is the computer itself. You program it and whatever you program in—it does. It takes in data, processes it, and creates behaviors. It is the place where most of our daily activities reside: 90 percent according to Waldron.

"Like driving to work the same way every day and automatically knowing exactly where to go and never making the conscious choice to turn, or slow down?" I ask.

"Yes, grasshopper," he tells me with a smile. "Just like driving."

A few important notes on the subconscious. Most golfers don't even believe that they have a subconscious mind. If you don't believe Waldron, take a poll at the driving range. Okay. The other thing to remember: Your swing is an invisible manifestation of your subconscious.

Which brings us to the subtle preconscious. Here I begin to get a bit hazy. There are elements of both the conscious and subconscious minds at work. You could say that it's semi-voluntary. Sex, dancing, many aspects of sports, and fistfights all come from the subtle mind. It's feeling your hands as opposed to seeing them.

The best mind state is the creative unconscious. This is where miracles happen. It's why Tiger pretty much kicks everyone's ass.

"Tiger has an aura," Waldron says. "He understands and can access all levels."

This is psychic power, mind over matter. It's high-level shit. When you hole out a chip, sink a long putt, or paint a picture that flows directly from your mind to the canvas—that's the creative unconscious. For guys like you and me—it's pretty much magic. For Tiger, it's normal.

The goal here is to imprint a better swing on my subconscious. Thus, we turn to Neurolinguistic Programming.

NLP blends Gestalt therapy, hypnosis, and some other psychological stuff. The important practical concern is finding a way to program things into one of the three sensory channels—visual, kinesthetic (feel), and auditory.

Luckily, I'm a feel guy. In the visual channel, you can process 10 bits of info per second. The auditory, 4 to 7 bits. Feel—and I'm pretty proud of this—20 bits. With the understanding that the port of entry into my sensory world is the one that processes information the quickest, Waldron runs me through numerous drills that will impact my balance and help me feel my way to a better swing.

Using the Stanislavski Method, which underlies Method Acting, Waldron asks me to hit from a variety of intentions. Like De Niro preparing for a role, I hit from both commitment and from courage. I am better at commitment. Despite my feel-channel tendencies, I must say that neither was easy. When I am asked to add "comfort" to "commitment," I shank one really badly. For the rest of my life, Waldron says, I should have an intention for every shot I hit.

For balance he has me hit standing on one leg and then using only one arm.

In this regard, Waldron has no idea whom he's messing with. If nothing else, my ability to demonstrate a mastery of a completely impractical and useless skill knows no bounds. Therefore, when I am like a metronome, knocking lovely, arcing shots out there with one hand or on one foot, Waldron is a bit puzzled. I totally suck, however, at hitting with my eyes closed.

Balance, we decide, should be my secondary focal point. Target first. Balance second. Simple as that.

"All bad shots are primarily caused by a loss of balance," Waldron tells me. "Hogan practiced balance over and over."

We also do the kung fu drill, which Nicklaus did as a kid, though I can't imagine it was called the kung fu drill back in Columbus, Ohio, during the 1950s. Here you basically try to remain flat-heeled, with your feet as pigeon-toed as you can get them. Your feet are your focal point. This is also the case with the Bobby Jones drills, where you use a waist-to-waist swing, often with your eyes closed, and focus on feeling how your weight distributes itself. The goal is to keep it in the middle.

Then came the Jug McSpaden drill—which changed my life.

Here's the backstory. Harold "Jug" McSpaden was one of the Gold Dust Twins on the PGA tour during the 1940s. The other was Byron Nelson. Early on, McSpaden was missing the cut at lots of tournaments and realized it was because his arms, not his body, were guiding his swing.

McSpaden returned to his farm one winter and did the drill outlined below 200 times a day in order to get rid of what Waldron calls "the pernicious effects" of the arm swing. That following summer, he began a long streak of being the guy who always finished second to Nelson or Hogan.

My description is not precisely as Waldron taught it to me, but it will give you the basics.

Stand at address. There should be no ball, nor should you ever hit a ball while doing this drill. Then do as follows:

1. (for righties; lefties should do the reverse) In semi-slow motion, use your arms out and backwards so the clubhead is pointing towards 2 o'clock (as if you were standing on 6 o'clock). Your hands should remain about waist height. Then pause.

2. Lift upwards towards the top of your swing. Pause again.

3. Now coil as you turn your body to the right. Pause.

4. Release the club as if you were swinging.

Do it. Do it again. Do it 10 times, 50 times, or 200. You can pick up the pace, but basically, push away to 2:00, push your arms up, then coil to the right and let go.

It took patience and I felt like an idiot. Then there was the epiphany. Suddenly, my conscious mind began to understand. Chet was right. Waldron was right. I was doing something unnecessary to compensate. But, with the Jug McSpaden drill, I began to feel how my body actually was supposed to work when it hit a golf ball. When I hit step 4 and let go into my swing, no swing thought in the world could screw up what was happening—my body was uncoiling, my swing plane was round, and my hands were suddenly coming not from somewhere on the outside of the plane but, even in slo-mo, were automatically whipping downwards very close to my hips and thighs just like the diagrams in Hogan's *Five Lessons: The Fundamentals of Modern Golf.*

After I'd done the drill for some time, Waldron let me actually start hitting some balls. I was stroking it. For the first time in my life, I suddenly understood what a really good golf swing felt like. I was a machine. Towards the end I hit a monstrous 165-yard 7-iron into a two-club wind.

"Motherfucker," Waldron said, "you did that better than me. Yesterday your swing sucked; today it's good—Zen golf, right?"

o o o o

What followed was a dizzying four-week period during which I played the best golf of my life. I'd been doing my Jug McSpaden and my kung fu drills religiously. I decided that my intention would always be to hit the ball as best I could and let the chips fall where they may. I would put score in its place, as Waldron had advised me. The results were spectacular.

There was an 85, with 40 on the back at Glencoe. I followed this up with an 84 at Lake Michigan Hills while on vacation in southwestern Michigan. My first drive was huge, but wildly off to the right and behind some trees. Yet I stiffed a 7-iron to within 15 feet, from the rough. It went on like that. When I made a mistake, I still had confidence in my new, much improved swing. I shot a 40 on the front and was on the way to doing the same on the back until I started fitting myself for a green jacket on fourteen and had a few stupid doubles.

Each time that I played, I was able to blend Yellin's zone training with what I'd learned from Waldron. When I strayed, I always found my way back and quickly. All told, I played five rounds in those four weeks. Each was 86 or under. I am not certain that I've ever had that many rounds under 86 in a year, much less consecutively over the course of a month. I had taken the journey and I was playing the best golf of my life.

Then it all began to unravel.

First there was a 97 in the rain with my dad and uncle. I wrote it off, but was having night sweats about the fact that I couldn't "get abstract" anymore. I worried about the placebo effect. I did more Jug McSpaden, but things didn't feel the same.

I sank into the abyss shortly thereafter. It was a Friday and I played at Glencoe with three strangers, including a husband and wife. I was chasing a score, trying to get back to the guy who lived in the low and mid-80s just a week or so earlier. My intention was all fucked up.

I shot a 50 on the front. It was a bad 50. I couldn't let go of obsessing about my score. I was out of the feel channel. I was a karmic, cosmic, out-of-the-zone golfing mess. I started making conscious adjustments to my swing—based on what my anxiety-addled brain could remember from my time in Portland and Iowa. Suddenly, I was saying "seventeen" each time I swung. My mind, however, was completely out of sync with my body.

As I sat in my cart on the eighteenth tee, after a triple bogey 7 on the seventeenth, the husband came over to me. A genuinely pleasant and lovely guy, he smiled as he dragged his chubby body to my cart. Head in hands, and clutching my pencil as if I were about to create my own stigmata, I knew this wasn't going to go well.

"If it's any consolation," he said between puffs of a cigarette and after having just been outdriven by his wife for the hundredth time, "a 7 is a good hole for me. C'mon, it's not so bad."

Then he said it. "After all, it's only just a game."

Of course he was right. Of course it was only a game. It was also only a bad stretch. It was hardly a measure of who I was either as a golfer or as a human being.

He was also right in saying this for less philosophical reasons. That's because he sucks at golf and was consistently hitting the ball 30 yards shorter than was his wife, who sucks as well. No wonder this asshole thinks it's just a game.

I looked into the man's cherubic face with its kind smile. And it took every ounce of strength, character, commitment, and intention to refrain from beating him to death like a harp seal with my 6-iron, before shoving it up his ass and retrieving it through his mouth.

"I know," I said. "It's just a game."

When I returned home, I was disconsolate. It was one of those moments when people call their rabbi, their priest, or their therapist seeking wisdom, understanding, and relief. I ran up to my office and emailed Steve Yellin.

He responded almost immediately. "Ah-hah, the perennial pitfall. I've seen it for thirty years. There is a remedy."

We decided to talk on Monday.

Big Sky Buddha

Golf is a game to teach you about the messages from within, about the subtle voices of the body-mind. And once you understand them you can more clearly see your hamartia, the ways in which your approach to the game reflects your entire life. Nowhere does a man go so naked.

—Michael Murphy

FALL 2007. MISSOULA, MONTANA

I'd arrived home from my disastrous round at Glencoe in a foul mood. Just a few hours before I had believed that I was heading towards enlightenment via golf. True, I hadn't seen the burning bush as rendered by Mike Murphy, but I had tasted the sweet nectar of better golf and an improved outlook on life. I'd felt as if I was beginning to see the light. Though not effortless, I was experiencing and enjoying my life and golf game in ways that I never had before. I was firm in the belief that, like Buddha before me, I was going to understand the Four Noble Truths (the nature of suffering, the origin of suffering, the cessation of suffering, and the way)—and get a hold on my own suffering, which would eventually lead towards scores in the mid-70s and happiness the likes of which I can only imagine is felt by people like Matthew McConaughey.

But I was wrong. Like the Four Noble Truths, my journey was far more complex than I had hoped. After days and weeks of what felt like progress, it was as if I'd been struck by lightning and not in a good way. I had looked beneath the surface of my life and my game only to realize that the Four Truths have a subset known as the Noble Eightfold Path (right view, right intention, right speech, right action, right livelihood, right effort, right mindfulness, right concentration), which has its own sets of amendments, clarifications, and interpretations that resemble the federal income tax code. I was in a fog of confusion, bewilderment, and rage.

I had no idea how I was going to get out of this mess. Up to this point, however, I'd had nothing but success, and with that definitely came a greater sense of peace on all fronts. The better my game, the better I felt about everything. And it wasn't like spiritual materialism where I was just thinking, "Wow, happier, better putting, life is good." Instead, I was exhibiting at least some elements of Buddhist virtues like patience, caring, and compassion.

Now, for those of you new to Zen, here is a simple test as to whether you have your Buddha on or not: When faced with a challenge or adversity, do you take the opportunity to be a happy, well-adjusted person who can handle life's vicissitudes, or do you become a sullen dickhead? I like to think that I do the former. But as my golf meltdown continued to metastasize, I remembered that my greatest skill is an ability to mask the latter with a hail-fellow-well-met attitude. Now I was having trouble with even that.

I was swallowing hard every time my wife asked me to do something—change a diaper, clean the yard, get out of bed. All of these sounded like direct attacks on my character. My inability to hold it together hit critical mass one Saturday when I carried my two-year-old son into the kitchen and found an entire gallon of milk spilled on the counter.

"Fuck!" I yelled.

My son Teddy looked at me and deadpanned, "Shit!!"

My saving grace was that I'd been reading *Zen and the Art of Happiness* by Chris Prentiss. Though it took me some time to get past the fact that the author ran a rehab clinic named "Passages" in Malibu (can't they come up with better, more appropriate names like "Downeytown" or "Lohanistan"?) I found solace in this short, profound book. Prentiss's essential philosophy is that no matter what is happening your primary thought should be, "This is the best thing that could be happening to me in this moment." Prentiss illustrates this with the story of how he fell 100 feet into a ravine and was lying temporarily paralyzed, face down in wet mud, thinking he'd just won the lotto. If he could do that, I thought, I could handle struggling to break 100. There must be a reason for this pain I am suffering. It must be for my greater good.

Thus I decided to go ahead and try it—saying the words to myself when I stepped in a puddle on the way to the bathroom in the middle of the night, only to realize that it was a lake of urine left by our incontinent St. Bernard. And as I washed my foot in the sink, I said to myself over and over, "This is the best thing that could be happening to me in this moment." And in truth, it does take on a weird power. The more you say it, the more you believe it.

This phrase got me through to Monday when I talked to Yellin. Our conversation was brief. I was not alone, he said. Others had seen the mountaintop only to fall back into the abyss. There was a road back to the land of milk and honey. I needed to go back to the basics. I needed to get abstract as hell.

With that thought commingling in my head with the idea that all is for the best, I boarded a plane to Missoula, Montana, several weeks later for two days of golf with Printer Bowler, author of *The Cosmic Laws of Golf (and everything else)*, one of my favorite books in the genre. Bowler, I sensed, was a homespun philosopher who seemed to understand how to lead a meaningful, spiritual life on and off the golf course without losing an ounce of masculine credibility.

o o o o

To see Printer Bowler's picture on the University of Montana journalism school's Web site (he is an adjunct professor) is to witness the vision of a rough-hewn, Big Sky edition of your Pop Warner football coach—a ruddy-faced, blue-windbreaker-wearing mix of Anthony Hopkins and Clint Eastwood, with a slightly grown-out gray brush cut and intense grey-blue eyes. The man simply looks like the state of Montana.

When I arrived in the tiny Missoula terminal I found a somewhat older, slightly less ruddy guy in that same blue windbreaker—just as alive and intense, but more narrow and weathered.

We had dinner at my hotel and found that we shared many things. Political leanings, love of Seve Ballesteros, and a general sense that American culture is headed in a bad direction. But there were also differences. He'd grown up in tiny Scobey, Montana, and had served in Vietnam. I was raised in upper-middle-class suburban Chicago and whiled away the Reagan years chewing tobacco and drinking Old Milwaukee Light.

The next morning Bowler and I headed for the Ranch Club, a par-72 course with a 75.3 rating and a 128 slope. The sky was appropriately gigantic, the wind perfectly blustery, and the course remarkably beautiful, with supremely green fairways set off against tall golden prairie grass.

Somehow I had managed to regroup and regain some shaky sense of self and confidence. I was standing on the first tee staving off the thoughts of "Don't fuck it up," when I made what I considered to be a very mature and Zen decision. I put my driver back in the bag and grabbed my 3-iron, figuring that I'd get it out in the middle and not suffer too badly for it on a 400-yard par-4.

"You didn't come all the way to Montana to tee off with your 3-iron, did ya?" he said in a friendly bark. His comment was a terrific summary of the dichotomy that I find so confounding about this melding of golf and spirituality. On the one hand, he was telling me "Hey, no one is watching and in the grand scheme of things it doesn't matter if you hit it out of bounds— you are a free and sentient being on this planet, play by your own rules, go for it—live, damn it, live!!!" And on the other, he had a foot straight in the world of American masculinity: "Don't be a pussy, hit your goddamn driver." These are comments that seem diametrically opposed somehow—the philosophy of nontraditional spirituality and stick-it-up your-buddy's-ass manliness—but from him it worked. It was a comment completely devoid of bullshit. Yet, it's a question that addles my brain: What is the balance between caring and not caring? How do you care, yet throw caution to the wind at the same time? Gain control by giving it up?

I grabbed my driver and anxiously knocked one out 230 down the middle and bogeyed the hole. I doubled the next two and was 5 over after three, thought it should have been 6, as I'd tripled the par-5 second, but Printer converted it to a 7 via the equitable scoring method.

The second was one of those holes that you have bad dreams about. A foursome—resplendent in Callaway and Nike, with gleaming square-headed drivers and new Vokey wedges—let us play through and sat on the tee watching while I made an ass of myself. The hole was long and intimidating: somewhat downhill, with a narrow chute and ample opportunity to fuck up in every direction. I seized each and every one. My tee shot landed on some barren earth, sidehill away from me to the right of the fairway. I slashed at it and hooked a 4-iron back into the fairway—kind of—and still had 200 yards left to get into the green. I hit a moderately decent 2-iron in, with no follow-through to speak of; thus it wound up slicing to the right, over the green and into a nasty trap, where my adventure began. Off the hardpan and with the green at about shoulder height, I clanked a wedge shot off the face of the trap, up in the air, and into another trap about 3 feet further towards the fairway, from which I did the same thing back into virtually the exact spot from where I'd hit my first wedge. With both shots, I could feel a vibration run through the club, up my arms, and down my spine. It was the vibration you felt on the first day of little league practice in 40-degree April weather when you shanked off a fastball with an aluminum bat.

I was running through the excuses in my head as I stood over my sixth shot. I was intimidated by the guys watching. I was rushed. I was concrete rather than abstract. My clubs were slipping in my cold hands. My wife's cat was sick. You know the drill. When I failed to get the ball out of the trap once more, the hole—12 feet away—seemed as distant as Pluto. My next swat hit the lip and took one of those great undeserved bounces straight up and then onto the fringe of the green, rolling very close to the hole. Close enough that I couldn't miss my putt—which mercifully Printer gave me.

After that, however, I settled down and finished the front with a 46 to his 47. Damn, I thought, I'd played like shit and I was one up on a guy who knew all about golf, life, and the cosmic laws that govern both.

I stood on the tenth feeling much, much calmer than before. Printer teed off and I made note of his swing. He's in his mid-sixties and somewhat slight. He isn't a big hitter, but his irons go as far as mine—and I outweigh him by a good fifty pounds. His shots make almost no noise. They say that Sam Snead's irons sounded like the door of a Rolls-Royce being slammed. Mine are loud as well, but never like a Rolls. More like a Buick on good shots, and akin to a Yugo being sideswiped by a Gremlin on the bad ones. From a narrow stance, he has a compact swing and takes divots in front of the ball—something Waldron insisted was the mark of a well struck shot. I, by contrast, almost never take up dirt, a fact that I tell Printer after picking a 6-iron shot clean without disturbing a blade of grass.

"You're a sweeper," he said. "Nothing wrong with that." Printer then told me about seeing 1987 Masters Champ Larry Mize play in Montana. He's a sweeper too. Though I would prefer a comparison to Snead, Seve, or Ernie Els, I was glad there is precedence for a sweeper to play great golf.

Both of us were playing better. We suffered our share of biblical woe, yet there were also moments of remarkable golf, such as a 20-plus-foot putt that Printer canned as if it were a tap-in.

"That was a Magic Triangle Putt!" he said in exultation.

"Absolutely!! Magic Triangle Putt!!" I said with authority. And though I've read his book at least twice, I had no idea what a magic triangle putt actually is.

o o o o

That evening back in my room, I looked up the magic triangle, which Printer learned in the service when an instructor taught him an unorthodox way of shooting his pistol. Rather than remembering technique, he was told to forget it. Instead, the soldiers were to imagine "a perfect triangle formed by the imaginary lines connecting [their] hand, eye, and target." This, they were told, would provide "automatic, precision hand-eye-target coordination."

It was in many ways a practical, modern-day retelling of a story about Arjuna winning an archery contest in which he and other great marksmen were asked to put an arrow through the eye of a fish that sat atop a tall pole, 130 yards away. His competitors came close, but none had hit the eye. When asked what they saw, the others noted all manner of things, the sky, the fish, the pole. When Arjuna went last, he was, one might say, a bit more "target focused." "I see the eye of the fish," he said, then put the arrow right through it.

The magic triangle is about a lot of things. It's about letting go and allowing things to happen without pressure. It's about intense concentration and the ability to lock onto what is important. It's about clearing away all of the bullshit and simply doing what you are there to do—without mental interference.

I also think it's about one of the key elements that rightfully underlie the golf-and-spirituality movement. It is the idea that you or I can stand 180 yards from a target holding a crooked piece of metal and—without benefit of some understanding of the physics and dynamics of how I ought to get the ball to the green—simply by feel and intention hit a dimpled ball to within 5 feet of a small hole that we are aiming for. While that is what we want to do on a golf course, it is also nothing short of a miracle. It is a pure expression of the magic inherent in the mind-body connection—my brain tells my body to do something that, when examined in practical terms, is patently insane. Then it works. As Printer later said to me, "Intention is important. You get an idea, you follow it, then you let it go. Golf is a great exercise in self-realization that way."

At the same time, however, we both realize that the power of golf to help us manifest the intentions of our best selves has been somewhat co-opted. It has also become—in Michael Murphy's words—"mystery school for Republicans." Essentially, a good way for well-off middle-aged guys to dabble in a bit of on-course self-improvement and faux spiritual depth while they wait for a sequel to *Who Moved My Cheese?* And I love well-off middle-aged guys. I grew up in a family full of them. They are my people.

The idea behind *The Cosmic Laws of Golf (and everything else)* was in many ways high concept—using the accessible game of golf to express certain truths that govern the universe and our lives. Golf was the vehicle to work a bit of nontraditional philosophy into the mainstream.

The cosmic laws break down like this:

#1. Law of Polarity—The idea that there must be balance in the universe. That nature abhors a vacuum, and Newton's law of motion that every action must have an equal and opposite reaction. Thus yin must have yang. Jack must have Arnie. Shields must have Yarnell.

This applies to golf; how, you may be asking. Well, let's just say that the guy who swings hardest doesn't always hit longest—and that the more you give up trying to control your shots, the more they reflect your intention for them. Got it? Let go, trust your swing—and the larger concept that the universe wants you to be happy—and enjoy the results.

#2. Law of Attractions—Basically, we create our own world, a concept in which one witnesses the rare coming together of Mohandas Gandhi (be the change that you want to see in the world) and Seve Ballesteros (you are what you believe you are).

Thus, how you view your game, each shot, every putt, creates in some way what will happen to you. Simply put, after you shank that second shot into the woods, do you a) figure out the calmest, most relaxed, safest way to get yourself out of jail, or b) grind your teeth to stubs while trying to hit a 2-iron shot off of a tree root and through a narrow passageway guarded by hundreds of branches?

#3. Law of Perceptions—Very much related to the Law of Attractions, but this chapter holds the distinction of being the only time in the history of golf literature that an author has quoted Marcel Proust. But it's just that kind of book.

"The real journey of discovery," that rascally Frenchman once said, clearly anticipating fellow countryman Jean Van de Velde's meltdown at the 1999 British Open, "consists not in seeking new landscapes, but in having new eyes."

Bottom line here, in life or with your 4-iron: Do you see the sand traps, or the clear path to the green? Do you put out positive thoughts or negative? Do you lie face down paralyzed in the mud and think it's the best thing that could be happening in that moment, or do you worry that any minute someone will start cranking Supertramp's "Breakfast in America" as well?

#4. Law of Intentions and #5. Law of Commitment—You cannot change your life or your golf game unless you are really serious about it. You need to find your true voice, which will never beat itself up over a chili-dipped pitch. You need to listen to that voice—and do so over and over again until it is second nature, which manifests itself as #6, the Law of Spontaneity.

#7. Law of Acceptance—Printer tells me a bit about this on the back nine. Years back he had an astrological reading, after which he made a list of all of the people, and things about himself, at which he was angry. He then forgave each and every person, including himself, which resulted in a gigantic clearing of mental space and negative thought.

I made a note to try this myself, while simultaneously believing that this kind of thing works for other people. Not me. I also wondered if I could afford enough paper to compile such a list.

In the end, the Cosmic Laws are telling us that golf, and much else that we undertake in life, is a way to let go, explore ourselves, and find the truth.

"That's the scariest thing—our real self," he tells me.

o o o o

Back at the Ranch Club, on eighteen, I crack my drive long and a bit left, but it was sitting up nicely in good position for a 5-iron approach from 160 into a green that's protected by a big pond abutting its left-front border.

I have played much more steadily on the back and have rattled off one of those strings of pars where suddenly you start thinking, "It's a simple damn game; I drive it, I hit it again, then I putt twice, and par is easy." I've been paying no attention to my score, just my individual shots and our conversation. Printer is a good distraction as the winds kick up, the sky grows dark, and it suddenly becomes cold.

I begin telling Printer about how I'm going to hit the easy 5-, rather than the 6-. Feeling supremely relaxed, I conjure images of a few high, arcing mid-irons I'd hit earlier in the day. Yet somehow at the forefront of my conscious mind there is an image that supersedes everything: In big, bright lights I cannot escape the number 42. And I am not thinking of Jackie Robinson.

There are some swings where you don't know what went wrong. There are some swings where you do know what went wrong. Then there are swings that are inexplicably horrific, the aftermath of which feels like a car accident. This was one of those swings. If I had to analyze what happened, I'd say that my legs may never have moved, that I hit about 4 inches behind the ball and deep into the turf, and that I nearly decapitated myself with my follow-through. The ball traveled 40 yards on a double bounce and wound up inches from the OB (out of bounds) stake on the left.

From 120, I stand and am somehow able to detach myself from needing to make a good shot. In some way I don't care, and worry whether or not this is good not caring, or bad not caring. I pull out my wedge and land a half-decent shot that clunks on the green about 12 feet short. My par putt is beautiful. I read the break perfectly from a glance and I am bold. I go for it and watch my ball grab the right edge but fail to fall down, sliding instead 4 feet past the hole. I will not be shooting 42. Shaken, I two-putt from there and slide in with a 44. Printer bogeys.

As we walk off of the eighteenth, Printer shoots me a cock-eyed smile.

"Well," he says in a cheerful growl that rumbled like a metal rake on dead grass, "that was a cathartic little workout." He sighs and laughs. "Shit!"

Final tally—Karp 46/44: 90; Bowler 47/42: 89. Cosmic laws take Jewish angst by one stroke.

o o o o

That night Printer had me over for steaks. We got to talking and I learned his life story. His father had been a hard-ass former Marine who operated his home like a military base. The Bowlers owned the local newspaper and radio station; Printer's dad had much wisdom to offer. One night as he sat silently at the table, he turned to his son, and said, "Do you know what the best business in the world is?" Printer shook his head. "Getting relief," said his father. Point well taken.

After college the government offered Printer an all-expenses-paid vacation in Southeast Asia, where he worked in psychological operations, dropping leaflets on villages that were going to be bombed shortly thereafter.

As we stand in the kitchen discussing this, tears well up in his eyes. "We were just killing these people," he says. Shortly thereafter he says that his experiences in Vietnam were an example of the law of polarity. We can't know good if we don't know evil.

That experience was part of a process in which he woke up and began to live consciously. Washed out with the world in which he'd grown up, the organized lifestyle, the Horatio Alger promise of America—working hard equals success—Printer got out of the military and moved to San Francisco, where he did not become a hippie as much as he started becoming himself.

"Things happen when you're ready," he says. "I was ready. I began to see [that life] was bullshit. The real powers weren't doing that. That's when I bailed and started my second life. I wanted real knowledge."

He began seeking "real knowledge." Thus, he began exploring "the pure shit." Not bothering with religion or man-made creations, he went in search of the source.

There was Hermes' *Emerald Tablet*, an ancient document which was in part the basis for some of both Isaac Newton's and Carl Jung's work. There was the Count of St. Germain, who (I truly could not do this justice) Wikipedia says has been "variously described as a courtier, adventurer, charlatan, inventor, alchemist, pianist, violinist, and amateur composer, but is best known as a recurring figure in the stories of several strands of occultism—particularly those connected to Theosophy, where he is also referred to as the Master Rakoczi or the Master R." It is claimed that St. Germain lived for centuries and was actually Christopher Columbus, Francis Bacon, Plato, and Merlin, among others. I will refrain from making the gratuitous Shirley MacLaine reference here out of respect for Printer and because, quite frankly, I love Shirley MacLaine. Ultimately, the general conclusion is that he was an "ascended master." And in the spiritual world, or pretty much anyplace else, it doesn't get much better than that.

Another big component of the Bowler influence lexicon is G. I. Gurdjieff—a Sufi master who lived from 1866 to 1949 and wrote a book entitled *Life Is Real Only Then, When 'I Am.'*

Gurdjieff's father, Printer tells me, wanted to educate him to be as fully alive as humanly possible, thus sending him out as a young man to experience all kinds of new and challenging situations where his mind would be forced to adapt in order to survive. Thus making his mind continually drawn to the present.

As we sit in his kitchen Printer tells me about how Gurdjieff once lived in the Middle East, where he opened a fix-it shop despite having no knowledge of how to fix anything. Instead, relying on the ideas that a) he could do it and b) whatever he needed was always there, he learned how to repair virtually anything and made a barrel of money.

In his own life, Printer tried to follow Gurdjieff's lead when his toaster broke. Taking the entire thing apart, he spent days trying to find out what was wrong. Every piece, however, seemed to be operating properly. Nothing was wrong. Flummoxed, he stuck with it until days later he found a tiny copper connection that was burned ever so slightly, filed and smoothed that piece, and put the toaster back together.

"What was important," he tells me, "was the process."

o o o o

On day two, at the Canyon River Golf Club, the magic triangle is laying a bunch of greens to waste. Printer opens up 4 over after five holes, then birdies the par-5 sixth in textbook fashion, drive long and straight, a cannon-shot fairway wood, a nice wedge in, and the magic triangle kicking in a 10-footer.

I go double, double, double, but par four and birdie five, a hole that I will never forget. It's a 414-yard par-4 with a long arcing dogleg left and down to a small green that offers death to those who are over. Even though it's October, the weather is warm and the sun is burning my neck and ears. After a nice drive, maybe 240 and down the middle, I stand over a 170-yard downhill shot with the wind at my back. It feels like a 6-iron to me. I pull the club, take two easy practice swings and—with a remarkably clear mind—proceed to hit a ball that I know is bound for glory the second I make perfect contact. As it hits about 10 feet directly past the hole, I have complete confidence that I will sink my putt. Which I do, drilling it straight to the center of the cup without a moment of doubt. In that moment, I realize the golfer and person that I can be when I don't think so damn much.

Printer closes the front with another birdie on the par-5 ninth. I am at 45. He is at 38. In this moment, albeit briefly, I realize the futility of my competitive spirit and gladly give up attaching my self-worth to my score on this day.

"Desire," Printer says at one point, "is the root of all suffering."

He pauses for a moment, drags on one of the Marlboros he's trying to quit, and laughs. "Ah, who the fuck knows?"

We press on.

The back nine looks much like the front. I put together a bunch of bogeys, a few doubles, and a par. The highlight is my tee shot on a 220+-yard par-3, where relying completely on instinct, I pull my 2-hybrid out and hit one of the best-feeling shots of my life, which bites at the back of the green 10 feet or so beyond the hole. Yes, the wind was at my back. But, it doesn't matter, even when I three-putt. I am playing based on feel, which I'm realizing is the only way to live or play golf.

Printer is 2-over heading into fourteen, a par-3 which he triples. He follows this with a birdie on fifteen, a par on sixteen, and another birdie on seventeen. The law of intention and the magic triangle are very, very good to him on this day. He has birdied four holes and is at 72 heading into the par-5 eighteenth.

It is hard to describe how ugly that hole was. I scramble my ass off to double bogey. Printer, on the other hand, has a "Tin Cup Moment." He is beset by what he calls *daemons*, "entities [thought-forms] we create, individually or together by nurturing a thought or idea until it seems to take on a life of its own. They become part of our being and influence the way we think, see and act."

And those daemons are waiting for Printer when he arrives at eighteen. His tee shot sucks, and so does his second shot. The smooth, compact swing now has a bit of Arnie-on-a-bad-day happening. It goes on like this pretty much until the moment he drops it into the cup for a triple-bogey 8, which puts him at 80, that fine line for better golfers, and to which

I aspire, between okay and having a sense that all is right with the world.

"Shit!!" he says, laughing and pissed at once.

Day 2—Karp: 93, Bowler: 80.

The better man won.

o o o o

When I got home, I emailed Printer to ask him about the best pieces of life and golf advice he'd ever received. This is what he told me.

Best (nontraditional) Golf Advice: "One of my favorite and most practical golf tips came to me intuitively one day: I imagined children swooshing up and down on playground swings. The rhythm of their movements—up and pause, gradually gather speed down and back up, and pause . . . etc.—appears to me as the perfect swing tempo. The still, relaxed moment at the top of the backswing, followed by a gradual increase in momentum as the club drops down toward the ball, allows the swing time to fall into place and move through the ball smoothly and powerfully.

"This tempo gives everything time to happen successfully. Your lower body naturally transfers weight to the left side and then you can pour on your turning power while the club starts falling back down on its path. In a word, a smooth and gradual takeaway, pause at the top, then turn smoothly and let the club descend as everything picks up speed. And forget that your hands exist so they can naturally hang back and quietly follow the turn and then whip into the ball unimpeded by tension and rigidity—that is how clubhead speed happens. With just a bit of practice, you can reach a point where there are no 'swing segments' or conscious positioning . . . you're just a kid having fun with a playground swing. Without fail, every time I keep this tempo I get the satisfaction of making a good, often great, golf shot."

Best Advice About Life and How to Live It: "The origins of all life's creations and experiences begin with ideas and images (thoughts). I may choose what thoughts I hold or reject from my mind. The ones I hold on to begin to manifest in my world. By my thoughts I literally create my world and how I relate to the world at large. It's as simple as that. It's also a lot of work."

And here were his final thoughts:

"My two triples are now forgotten except as I mention them here. Now there's a self-contradicting sentence if I ever wrote one."

CHAPTER 5

And on Your Deathbed You Will Receive Unconditional Confidence . . . Which Is Nice

Zen does not confuse spirituality with thinking about God while one is peeling potatoes. Zen spirituality is just to peel the potatoes.

—BRITISH PHILOSOPHER ALAN WATTS

FALL 2007. OJAI, CALIFORNIA

I am sitting on the patio of a café in paradise. The same paradise that was Shangri-La in Frank Capra's *Lost Horizon*. I am in Ojai, California, and—more specifically—the Ojai Valley Inn and Spa. I sit, hands folded in my lap, eyes open and softly focused just past my coffee cup, breathing in and out rhythmically through my lower belly at the instruction of Dr. Joseph Parent. His disciple and right-hand man, Ken, sits across from me, Zen Golf hat off, hands in lap, staring softly forwards and breathing.

It is 11:00 A.M. We move our focus to become aware of our field of vision. We don't move our eyes. We just test the limits of what we can see when we are still: side to side; up and down; near and far. Then we close our eyes and focus on what we hear. What do we hear? We don't need to label it, but we need to be aware. What noises come from the course? The birds in the trees? The wind? The road? Behind us? The kitchen? Other patrons?

Yes, I am meditating on a patio, 10 feet from other people who are not here to meditate, but are actually doing what people do at cafés: drinking coffee, grabbing an early lunch, cooling off with an Arnold Palmer. And maybe it's because I'm tuned in to myself, or, more likely, it's because I'm in Southern California and people must do this shit all the time, but I'm decidedly not self-conscious and nobody even seems to notice that we are meditating. In public. At a golf course. Of course we are. Who doesn't?

Before we started, Dr. Parent told me that we shouldn't label this exercise "meditation" per se. At least he doesn't like to call it that. When you meditate, most people (or at least most men) get a derisive look on their face and imagine—at best—Richard Gere and the Dalai Lama and—at worst—every soy latte-sipping, Birkenstock-wearing asshole who became a Buddhist or vegan in the last month and can't stop telling you all about it. Meditation can lead one to believe its purpose is to zone out and banish all thought. Goal One is counterproductive and Goal Two is illusory.

"Our mind is clear only when we are asleep but not dreaming," Dr. Parent tells me. "Our mind is always full. But we can change what it's full of. It's better to be full of perception and the present moment than thoughts of the past and future."

I'm with him. Awareness is about waking up and being quietly alive to and in the present moment. Being where you are and really being there.

After we focus our awareness on the feelings of warm breeze on our faces, our bodies in our seats, and other physical sensations, Dr. Parent asks Ken and me to slowly, thoughtfully—and deliberately—lift our drinks to our lips and take a sip. It's the most attention I've ever paid to a cup of cold coffee in my life and I taste every ground of every bean while noticing how my mouth and lips move automatically to drink it.

As I sit there, sipping the cold coffee for the second time, I am suddenly struck by the irony that this golf course–based awareness practice is the most instantly effective bit of meditation that I've ever done. My thoughts existed, but didn't trouble me. My body let go. I felt completely there, grounded, relaxed, and aware. Historically, I've needed to smoke a considerable amount of something a bit less spiritual to get this grounded and relaxed, but the result of that was the opposite of heightened awareness and was generally marked by watching late night reruns of *Family Feud* and waking up with an empty bag of chocolate chip cookies on my chest.

Awareness practice is really the first step to becoming a Zen master of any kind. There is awareness, then there is recognition of our self-defeating behaviors, and finally, undoing. You need the awareness for the recognition. You need the recognition for the undoing. Once it's all undone, you have the world by the ass. But, by that time, I assume, it doesn't even matter to you that you have the world by the ass, or something like that. Anyway, awareness is a good place to start.

o o o o

That morning I'd met Ken at the range. A tall, lanky guy in his mid to late forties, Ken had sent me an email the week before that confirmed our meeting but noted, "As with all phenomena, these plans are subject to the vicissitudes of impermanence." And this day, those vicissitudes came in the form of a golf magazine editor also in town to take a lesson from Dr. Parent. Though things were going to be done on the fly, Ken assured me that Dr. Parent would give me more than my money's worth.

When he comes over to say hi, Doc Parent is not what I'd feared he'd be: an arrogant, cocksure huckster with glittering $$ signs for eyes and © stamped on his forehead. Instead, he's a sturdy, thoughtful, soft-spoken guy in his mid-fifties who is a lot like a friend of your uncle's who happens to have become enlightened.

Doc tells Ken to have me hit some wedges, 7-irons, and 4-irons, to see if we can pick up a "dispersion pattern." The general idea behind this seems nonspiritual. If I hit ten to fifteen shots, we can see how far the bad ones go as opposed to the good, and generally how far left or right of the target they fall. Thus, my 7-iron tends to travel anywhere from 142 to 155 yards and tends to drift 10 to 20 yards right of my target. Far fewer go left, and those that do land closer to the flag. This inspires Doc to suggest that I start telling myself—out loud—"It's OK to be a little more open to the target." Which I do. Though not out loud.

There is also an unspoken moral and spiritual component to this. It's about how we lie to others and ourselves. It's the endless big dick contest that golf can become. Where we are 160 yards from the green and pull out that 7-iron because several years ago—with the wind at our backs, having just washed down a PowerBar with a Red Bull and hitting downhill—we hit it 162. In our minds, that's us, the guy with the 162-yard 7-iron, even though we've only done it a few times in a life consisting of hundreds of 7-irons. It's the height of self-delusion and unconsciously bending the truth to satisfy our egos. It's the same instinct that causes us to give ourselves that 6 instead of a 7 on that par-5, because if we'd played the course before and knew the putt was going to break that way we'd have lined it up differently and knocked it down. So, it's only fair to take the 6, right?

Not immune to this condition, I tell Doc that when I hit it well, I can knock my 7-iron out there 160. He quickly leads me back to reality.

As I hit, Ken asks me to rate my "inner state" on a scale of 1 to 5, 1 being when I sense the most interference (anxiety, swing thoughts, unquiet mind chatter) and 5 being when I feel the least. He tells me to give these scores regardless of the result, but it's hard not to. I even start creating new scores like 3+, which baffles Ken and whose meaning I can't explain.

After the range, we move to the putting green where I do something called "putting to nowhere." Basically you do just that: Drop some balls on the green and putt, but not toward the hole or anything else. You just putt—to nowhere. And bizarre as it sounds, the exercise is extremely freeing, as is another tip from Doc's *Zen Golf*, in which he discusses having a big mind.

Here is how that goes. Most of us have small-minded tunnel vision when we stand over a putt. Our entire universe exists in a narrow band of grass between our ball and the hole. We are hole bound. We are trying to "hole" our putts, instead of "making" them. In big mind putting, we open up our consciousness, make our brains and hearts more spacious, taking in the entire green (behind the hole, to the sides) in all of its undulating glory. The result is that we remove a giant pole from our asses and start sinking putts we didn't sink before, in part by making the hole itself a less significant focus of our attention. It's just another place on the green, albeit the one place where we do want our ball to end up.

I'd been messing around with this concept for a few months, making sure to always look past the hole and take in the entire area, just making myself aware that it existed. I also gave up trying to putt the ball in the hole and focused on hitting it in a way that felt good. The chips then fell where they fell and more often than in the past, my ball fell in the hole.

o o o o

To those who don't know his work, Doc Parent is the Dr. Big in the world of nontraditional, Eastern-tinged methods of improving your golf game. His influence in this area is so ubiquitous that in the past two months I'd played with at least three complete strangers of wildly differing ability, all of whom were clearly under the spell of *Zen Golf*. It was easy to tell because after a bad shot, each of them stood back, took a breath, and said—out loud—"Interesting . . ." This is part of Doc's PAR approach: Preparation, Action, and Reaction. This falls into the reaction category, a way of not beating yourself up for bad shots. Instead, you simply observe them as part of the rich pageant of Whitmanesque multitudes that make up your golf game.

Like Richard Lewis, Sandy Koufax, Jesus, and myself, Doc was born Jewish. Yet, when he tells you his story, Buddhism seems as if it were an inevitability.

His father was an engineer at Johnson and Johnson, living in the New Jersey suburbs with a station wagon, a dog, 2.3 kids, and a white picket fence. Doc was a three-sport athlete who loved to play golf and had an interest in spirituality that ranged from attending church with friends to inviting the Mormons into the house to actually make their sales pitch.

While an engineering major at Cornell in the early 70s, Doc was walking across campus one day when he began to have an internal conversation with himself about life and the future. He began asking himself questions that were answered without conscious thought. "What do I want to do?" was the first. "I want to teach," was the answer. "Teach what?" he asked himself. "Math," his thinking mind answered. But, letting his intuition take over, Doc realized that he was more interested in "people and why we do the crazy things we do."

By crazy, he didn't mean psychosis or the stuff that puts you in the mental hospital. Doc was talking about the things that put us all in mental hospitals of our own making: the chatter in our minds, the ways we get in our own way, or what he calls "self-destructive behaviors."

Immediately heading for the psychology department, Doc filled out a change-of-major form, which included the question: "Why do you want to major in psychology?"; to which he responded, "To find out why I want to major in psychology."

Like many of his generation Doc didn't want to follow in his father's path to the burbs. Unlike most of them, he actually continued into uncharted territory.

While a graduate psychology student at the University of Colorado, Doc fell in with the Shambhala warriors and their leader, Trungpa Rinpoche, as well as his disciple Vajra Regent Osel Tendzin (also know as Thomas Rich, Jr.), who became Doc's teacher. Over the years, Doc had encountered various gurus, all of whom had promised "the answer" or "the way." But, he wondered, how could so many know the way, yet each of them have a different path and definition of their end goal. Buddhism was different. It was familiar, like an old friend. Answers were not offered, but a tool-laden path was provided to find one's own version of those answers that reside within each of us.

That aspect of Buddhist philosophy, the idea that the answers and the sources of happiness are all within us, is a central tenet of nearly all golf-and-spirituality literature, from the idea of the "authentic swing" in *The Legend of Bagger Vance* to Doc's use of the ancient story of the Golden Statue in *Zen Golf*.

Here's the basic story line: An ambitious young man inherits a treasured clay statue from his family. When he achieves prosperity he has it covered over in gold. But as time passes, the gold chips away and he is frequently in need of re-covering it with gold again and again at considerable cost—all to maintain "the gold façade of his statue."

Some time later, the young man, with a mix of pride and shame (as the gold covering is chipping once again) shows his grandfather the statue. The older man grabs a wet cloth and begins to wipe away the gold and eventually the clay, underneath which is a statue made of solid gold.

"Many years ago," the grandfather says, "the statue must have fallen in the mud and must have become covered with it. . . . Underneath the covering your statue has been solid gold from the very beginning. You never needed to put more gold on to cover the clay. Now that you know what its nature really is, all you have to do is gently remove the clay and you'll reveal the gold statue you've possessed all along."

The essential message of the story is that all human beings possess an essential goodness, which we spend considerable time papering over with home renovations, Humvees, plastic surgery, and plasma TVs, or, in the case of most golfers, that new square driver or heavy putter. These are the things we think and hope will make us happy. But in reality all we need to do is wipe away that outer layer and we find that happiness and wholeness were always there to begin with. One doesn't need to be meditating to see how this applies to our golf game. If we got out of our own way and just played to play, we'd be fine and—more often than not—the results would take care of themselves.

In the late 1970s, Doc hooked up with a golf pro named Ed Hanczaryk, who had an interest in Buddhism. Doc was a Buddhist with an interest in golf. "We played a lot of Shambhala golf together," Doc says of their friendship, which led him to giving lessons that combined golf, psychology, and Buddhism at several clinics. The students ate it up. Thus, in the 80s, while Doc taught stress management techniques, he also began giving Zen golf lessons to a kid who was about to turn pro. This led to students on the developmental tour, which he followed to the PGA, where he encountered Vijay Singh, who became his most famous student.

When I ask Doc what kind of stuff he helps the pros with he tells me that "the level of issues great golfers and high handicappers face are staggeringly similar. Even for the pros, interference comes up. Hazards become the foreground instead of the fairway."

The pros "think" about what a shot is for, rather than just thinking about the shot without its implications. For them it might mean millions in prize money. For the rest of us, it's about ego.

"Our ego is worth more than a million dollars," Doc says. Mine sure the hell is.

When I ask whether he was intimidated by giving lessons to a maniacally prepared, twelve-hours-a-day-at-the-range work-aholic like Vijay—who was frequently #1 in the world before it became Tiger against everyone else—I get this:

"No, because I have unconditional confidence," he says matter-of-factly, with the air of someone who either possesses unconditional confidence or is doing a great job faking it. I'm not sure I've met anyone who feels this way. I, a master of uncondi-tional anxiety, am having a hard time relating.

Without thinking, I write the following in my notebook: "Unconditional confidence: Need to get some."

o o o o

Doc, Ken, the editor, and I tee it up on thirteen because a Scot-tish couple is going off ten. As the editor prepares to hit his drive, Doc gives him a pep talk about trusting your own instincts, tell-ing him that his first priority is to listen to the feeling in his gut.

"Then what does it mean if I just threw up in my mouth?" the editor asks, only half joking.

It's a longish par-4 and each of us hits a pretty nice drive, in play 220+ yards and with a reasonable shot to the green. Doc knocks his second into a greenside trap. Ken is short and left. The editor slams his ball wildly off course, short and way left. His pale skin turns boiling red.

"I loved your trajectory," Doc says, without even a hint of sarcasm. "And I like your angle to the green from there."

From about 190 and in the rough, I take out my 3-iron, more club than I need, dial it back a bit and with nice tempo send a high arcing shot over the trap guarding the right front side of the green. I'm on in 2. Doc asks what I hit. "My 3-," I tell him. He smiles, acknowledging in silence how I'd gotten out of my own way.

The others get on in 3 or 4 and face long putts. I wait patiently until I'm out. I look past the hole, get expansive, give up my interest in the result, line up, and knock it straight in from 15 feet.

"You 'made' that putt instead of 'holing' it, didn't you?" Ken beams.

"Uh-huh," I say, nodding as if I always birdie the first.

On fourteen, a 200-yard par-3, I hit my 3-iron on the green, while everyone else is either on the fringe or in the shit, like the editor, who is way left again. I three-putt for a bogey. Ken pars, Doc bogies as well. I stop tracking the editor's score.

At fifteen, I par, as does Ken. Doc and the editor either bogey or double again.

As I stand on the tee at sixteen, I begin to think, "After three holes I'm even par. The editor is at least 6 over. The best-selling author of *Zen Golf* is at least 3 over and I've got his disciple by a stroke."

Okay, in retrospect I realize that this isn't my best moment. For all of the Buddhism, Zen, Cosmic Law, and string theory I've encountered on this journey, I remain in silent competition with people who probably aren't competing with me at all. My million-dollar ego is on full internal display. It is pathetic if not completely shameful. I am a man in his early forties measuring his self-worth against others based upon three holes of golf. Add on the fact that Doc and Ken are "teaching" in this moment and might not be totally on their games as a result. But when it comes down to it, I can't help thinking, "I'm beating a guy who gave advice to Vijay!!"

It's a moment not unlike when you stand in front of the best-sellers table at Borders and are suddenly dumbstruck by the fact that a bloated old stoner like Andrew Weil is telling the world how to achieve Optimum Health—in eight goddamn weeks!!

It doesn't last. On sixteen, a downhill 203-yard par-3 with a gigantic cluster of bunkers across the front of the green, Doc announces that he's going to hit an 8-iron off the tee and has "pre-accepted" that he will likely bogey. He advises the editor to do the same. I believe Ken follows suit. I do not, pulling out my 3-iron and swinging like a cokehead on a three-day meth bender. I am 50 yards short in a shallow hole between several traps. After I barely hack my way out and wind up with a merci-ful triple bogey, I ask Doc, "How the hell do you hit out of a hole like that?" to which he replies, "You move your ball to a decent lie and hit it from there."

On seventeen, Doc laces his drive far left into some barren earth covered by nasty brush. The type of thing that would cause a less evolved golfer to implode. Doc looks up placidly. "I nut-ted that one, but I planned for a fade that never happened." And he marches on, a living embodiment of a quote from *Zen Golf*, which clearly applies to life beyond the fairways: "Never com-plain about anything—ever—not even to yourself."

At some point the editor hits a bad shot that takes a worse bounce off the cart path to god-knows-where. Chagrined to the point of turning purple he is calmed somewhat when Doc says, "You need to stop blaming yourself for things that are beyond your control." It's great advice, straight from the real Buddha, but you really don't hear it very often, do you?

I wonder where Doc was when I failed biology sophomore year.

The editor and Ken bail after eighteen, while Doc and I head to the front nine. On the first hole, a pissed-off couple arrives as we're about to tee off, aggravated that we are jumping in on them at the turn. Doc works some kind of Zen magic and suddenly they want us to take our time.

On the tee, I make two important decisions. 1) Fuck my driver. It has been causing me nothing but pain for more than a month and I'm going with my gut and teeing off with my Hogan #2 Hybrid. Off a tee, I hit it 220 and straight. I'm going to be satisfied with that. 2) I decide to try to let go of caring about my score for the rest of the day. Hey, if the scorecard in my head is right, I won or tied for best score on the first six holes anyway.

What follows is a mix of pars, bogeys, and doubles. I care, but somewhat less than usual. For a moment I come to the realization that nobody is keeping score and whether I'm 3 or 30 over, it shouldn't have much of an impact on the world aside from the fairways I hack up. It occurs to me that it makes little sense to define myself—and the next several hours of my life—by how I play this nonsensical sport.

Doc is great company and while we play he offers up the following:

As we head out on one hole, "Just trust the Force, Luke; we're here for exploration."

When I casually hit what is called an "anyways" in Zen golf parlance, he says, "I'd like to see a little more commitment on that one, OK?"

Before we tee off on a par-3 (which I wind up parring), he suggests that I "see it from the hole's perspective. Let the ball do its job."

And after I hit my best shot of the day, "There wasn't much Josh in the way on that one, was there?"

When we return our cart, Doc suggests that my goal ought to be more 4s and 5s on the "level of interference with my inner state" scale instead of more pars and birdies. We shake hands and he gives me directions to the Pacific Coast Highway for my drive back to Los Angeles.

o o o o

My first attempts at integrating the "more 4s and 5s" approach into my golf game and life are a mixed bag. A week after I returned, I played eighteen holes with a buddy who has a similar handicap but is a lesser athlete and golfer than I believe myself to be. As I've improved, his game has inexplicably done so at a maddeningly similar pace.

Here were the positives. I shot a 92 on a course that I rarely play. I had my version of what Tiger might refer to as his C game, as if he actually had anything but an A or B game. So, my bad rounds are more consistently mirroring what used to be my average rounds. I had no major breakdowns, even after four-putting a green that I reached in regulation. I realized that a piece of putting advice Doc had given me—about the way I positioned my club—was killing me, and stopped with about five holes to go. I guess you'd call that self-knowledge. Additionally, several times I stopped to remind myself that I should be playing for more 4s and 5s.

The downside? Well, I never was able to keep my brain on track for very long. The round pretty much happened to me, but not in a Zen way. Instead, I was unable to attain 4 or 5 on the mental interference scale, because I was refusing to slow down. The chatter in my brain put me at a 2 or 3 most of the time and I was unable to approach anything like awareness, let alone recognition or undoing. I guess this is probably the type of thing you need to practice. And, in the end, when my friend shot an 87, I felt belittled. Not good.

In my personal life, however, I used the same tricks to dial it back a bit and relieve myself of some unpleasantness. As I returned home at 11 P.M. on a Thursday evening, Mrs. Karp, large with child, told me that I looked like shit. I began to express how tiring it has been to travel so much, take red-eyes, drive from place to place, and have to be "on" when I'm with a partner or teacher. This elicited little sympathy. It was the classical marital "Do I look fat in this?" setup. But I caught myself and said, "No, I'm fine."

The marital stakes were taken up a notch two days later when Mrs. Karp told me that I was paying insufficient attention to her and hadn't offered up proper thanks for the fact that she looked after the kids while I was away. Before responding with my old standbys ("I'm not paying attention to you? What about me?" or the always sure to please, "Listen, you only feel this way because you're pregnant"), I breathed, cleared my mind, stepped back—at least mentally—and listened. Then I said, "You've been through a lot. You must be exhausted."

The results beat the crap out of sleeping in the guest room.

Equally successful was my ability to attain 4-to-5ness while taking my four-year-old to his weekly "mini-majors" baseball camp. When he stood up to hit from the left side, despite being a righty, I resisted the impulse to run up there and turn him around. And believe me, it was not a passing thing. I was terribly concerned that he'd forever be screwed up at the plate and mocked by his peers. But I sat there, became aware of my mental interference, recognized it, undid it a bit, and remembered that this moment would have little bearing on anything. In fact, I even remembered that his having fun and maybe learning something might be the most important things.

Now, I was aided in this by another father (in yellow golf shirt, madras shorts, and loafers that cost more than my Callaway irons), who was neither Buddhist nor above a 1 or 2 on the scale by which I was now measuring myself. I could empathize. I'd been there. He stood behind home plate the entire hour of practice. His activities were restricted to three things: 1) Talking on his cell phone. 2) Practicing his imaginary golf swing and doing some weird thing where he hooded his left hand and held it by his right ear while he swung. And 3) screaming the following things: "Come on, Matty. Focus up. Be ready. Remember it's your ball, go after it!!" while yet another pre-schooler takes six swings to hit it off of a tee. Or "C'mon, Matty. Take a good cut, buddy. Look at the ball. You didn't look at the ball. Focus up. Hit it." If they were alone and the sport was basketball and the child five years older, I can imagine him bouncing the ball off his head like Robert Duvall did to Danny Noonan in *The Great Santini*.

Clearly, he was putting layer after layer of gold on his and his son's statue. Guys like that make this Zen business a lot easier sometimes.

CHAPTER

6

The Bizarre Shit

*When I putt, my emotions collide like tectonic plates. It's left
my memory circuits full of scars that won't heal.*

—MAC O'GRADY

Then it was time for the bizarre shit. Or at least that's what
Coach Stephen promised when I arrived at the Columbus Airport during a February snowstorm.

There he was at baggage claim, tall and bald, with that beach-
volleyball-player/hipster-jazzman beard that ran from the lower
lip to the bottom of the chin, chipped black nail polish on the
thumb and forefinger of his right hand, and a gold hoop through
his left ear.

He was a walking advertisement for Renegade Mindset
Techniques (formerly Tap In Golf), his brand of instruction that
is based primarily on the Emotional Freedom Technique (EFT),

which—despite the fact that we'd all probably enjoy emotional freedom—doesn't quite market as well to the guys as something with the word *Renegade* in it.

As we drove through Jack Nicklaus's hometown, we got right into it. Stephen told me that he was a graduate of the California Institute of Integral Studies in San Francisco, whose motto is "higher education honoring the spiritual dimension of intellectual life," and whose two degree programs are professional psychology and consciousness transformation.

Stephen, I believe, studied integral counseling or energy psychology. Frankly, I was ready for a bit of anything that would help me find greater peace.

It had been a chaotic winter at the Karp household. After my trip to Missoula, I hung up the sticks and assessed my game and my life. Between the lesson with Yoni and my two rounds with Printer Bowler, I had gone from an 18- to a 15.6-handicap. Not bad, I thought. Not even a third of the way into this journey, I'd shaved more than two strokes off my game and, while I still had a ways to go, my existence was less anxiety ridden. Was I shooting for fully integrated, joyful, fearless—and a 2-handicap? You bet your ass. But the growing "absence of bad" was a step in the right direction and the journey, after all, is made up of little steps.

In early December my wife had given birth to our fourth son in eight years. As John Francis Karp came into the world, his mother had a copy of Raphael Shapiro's self-published *Mac O'Grady:The Rise and Fall of a Potential Golfing Superstar* clenched between her teeth. The irony was not lost on Mrs. Karp, as nearly all of my free time the past several months had been spent absorbing esoteric golf meisterworks that ranged from *Newton on the Tee* to *Gita on the Green*.

Over the years, I'd played golf with numerous men who had four children. Each and every one explained that once you went from man-to-man (two kids) to zone defense (three), it didn't matter how many more you had. I can safely say they were full of shit. My life is a constant blur of work, lunch making, homework, school drop-off's, diaper changing, and the breaking up of fights that border on Hagler versus Hearns— if Marvin and Tommy had come into the ring with broken Toys"R"Us light sabers.

Since my son's birth I wake each morning knowing only one thing: There are several important things that must be done that day that I will not do, nor will I even be aware of what those things are so that I might do them tomorrow. Yet, in some meditative way, I'm all right with that. I can remain somewhat calm in the midst of the storm. Fulfilling some adapted Buddhist version of Kipling's maxim about keeping your head when all about you are losing theirs. When it gets bad, I breathe and try to remind myself that I still have my health, my home, and my family. But, at the same time, the response in my brain is almost always, "Yeah, but for how long?"

Almost immediately after returning from the hospital, Mrs. Karp began dropping hints that I ought to stop canceling the appointments for my vasectomy. In particular she noted that I'd rescheduled one so that I could take my kids to a Chicago Blackhawks–Calgary Flames game. By February, these subtle hints involved me living over the garage. Thus, it was high time for me to drag my still potent self to Columbus for a golf lesson.

o o o o

Coach Stephen is what Margaret Thatcher used to call "an intense motherfucker." I say this with love and respect, as he's a terrific, intelligent guy who is fun to be with and not at all full of shit. But, he's got that energy that the truly healthy—and particularly the truly healthy that don't have kids—possess. His training methods are infused with what he calls a "need for speed." His healthy lifestyle is not something he lords over you, but you get the sense that everything he consumes is organic and that each bit of food, albeit delicious, has a precise purpose that it quickly fulfills when it enters the bloodstream, where his body maximizes the nutrients then dumps out the waste in neat little packages.

We drive to a restaurant where we are meeting Bill, a hypnotist and NLP expert, for breakfast. As we sit in a booth, Stephen and I discuss happiness, which gets us into a conversation about the book *The Geography of Bliss* in which writer Eric Weiner traveled the world seeking to find where the happiest people reside to unlock the key to their lack of ennui—only to discover that his answer was: Denmark. Yes, the Danes are the world's happiest nation. Why, you ask? Because they have the lowest expectations. Americans? Well, in the land of the free and the home of the grande-skinny-no-foam latte we suffer from what Weiner calls "the unhappiness of not being happy."

Unquestionably, I am among those who wonder several times each day whether I am happy, fully present, or free of anxiety. From the moment I wake up until I collapse at night, I am beset with thoughts about whether or not I am happy. On bad days, each moment is analyzed. The recurrent theme song running in the back of my mind is Tony Bennett's "Are You Havin' Any Fun?" which makes life sound pretty simple. And, I assume, it is for pretty much everyone but me—until I attend a suburban cocktail party where the two primary topics of conversation are home remodeling projects and the fact that everyone's gifted child isn't being fully challenged by their kindergarten curriculum. Quickly you realize that pretty much no one over thirty-five that owns property is having any fun.

Then Bill arrives. Like me, he is a father of four. Like Stephen, he has a shaved head. Like neither of us, he has a lipstick mark tattooed on the side of his neck and wears a suit with a black T-shirt underneath. When he orders a large glass of chocolate milk with his breakfast, I wonder to myself, "Is that what emotional freedom looks like? Chocolate milk for breakfast?"

When he was seventeen Bill met Tony Robbins, and then went to study NLP, did a bit of firewalking, the whole nine yards. He attended the American School of Hypnotherapy and earns a living putting that education to a variety of uses—weight loss, smoking cessation, and even that thing where he puts comedy club patrons under and makes them sing like opera stars and dance like chickens. Hypnosis, Bill tells me, is a tool that you can apply wherever you want.

After breakfast Bill follows Stephen and me to the international headquarters of Renegade Mindset Techniques. As we hit a stoplight in downtown Columbus, Stephen tells me that he once spent a good deal of time at a Japanese Zen monastery where nobody speaks. It is difficult to imagine Coach Stephen not speaking for a nanosecond, which he readily acknowledges. Yet, he also tells me that after four days of silence your mind quiets and the constant chatter subsides, then disappears. Some time thereafter, you get completely out of your head. You are drinking water when you are drinking water. You are walking when you are walking. Wherever you go, there the hell you are.

I try to think of a moment when I have felt this way. I cannot. Then I try to think of a moment where this would be possible. I cannot recall one. Finally, I consider that most of my nonwork time involves trying to decipher what is going on while at least two people are talking—at all times—about everything from farts to Power Rangers. As I sit in Coach Stephen's passenger seat, I am struck by the fact that my opportunity to be in silence for four days or more will come sometime in my early sixties.

Stephen's clients are junior golfers, desperate housewives, and a variety of athletes, including a few Ultimate Fighting Championship contenders. All of them want the same thing, he tells me. They want to be happy.

Like me, Stephen once sought such happiness through conventional talk therapy, which he was admittedly very good at. Each week he would identify pain, find its source, analyze it from every imaginable angle, and then go home none the happier.

"It's an interesting paradigm," he says. "It took me a long time to get over it."

But he did.

After that Stephen decided to cut out the middleman. He realized that our natural state is to be "in the zone." At first he tried to get his clients to try meditation. Quickly, however, he realized that he had "a compliance problem." Nobody wanted to sit for ten minutes, let alone two hours or entire days. That is when he found EFT.

Developed by a man named Gary Craig, EFT is the practice of tapping your meridians—the staple EFT move—to create a form of self-administered emotional acupuncture. The bottom line, according to the EFT Web site, is that "the cause of all negative emotions is a disruption in the body's energy system." Tapping can clear negative emotions. No therapy. No meds. No hours on the meditation cushion. Tap and be. That's the deal.

My history with this kind of stuff isn't particularly stellar, as many years back a hippie cousin and my wife persuaded me to join them at an introduction to, and indoctrination ceremony for, something called GeoTran, where a woman who looked like Barbra Streisand if she were a divorced yoga teacher, demonstrated how she could work with energy by circling her fingers around various body parts while reciting the numbers that corresponded with the area. Thus, "six, six" might be your stomach.

At one point she asked for volunteers—doubters—to come up, so that she could demonstrate the power of GeoTran. I have never raised my hand so quickly. She asked me to hold my arm out at 90 degrees and she tried to push it down, with little success. This, however, was before GeoTran, which consisted of her circling my shoulder joint with her fingers and saying, "two, two." She did this several times. Then she tried to push my arm down. I showed a grim determination that day, which I had never exhibited during a lackluster high school football career. She GeoTranned me some more. In fact, she GeoTranned me to death. Yet, nothing would or could make my arm move, certainly not GeoTran.

As I stood there grinning, she explained something about my having really bad energy and that it would take a lot of GeoTran to work out my problems. I laughed, only to look around the room to realize I needed to make a quick escape before I was pelted with natural fiber handbags and "Life Is Good" portable coffee mugs.

That was long ago. I was a different man. I wasn't ready for Coach Stephen then. Now, I was.

o o o o

Coach Stephen operates from a low-slung warehouse in Columbus where he and his wife run a personal training and sports performance business. He leads me into a small room with a massage table against a wall.

I sit in a chair. Stephen is facing me and we begin with a general clearing. This involves tapping with the fore and middle fingers of each hand on a pressure point/meridian located a few inches below the collarbone. EFT and Renegade Mindset are both all about the tapping. And before you dismiss it, the entire Oregon State University 2007 College World Series championship team tapped their asses off all season and through the playoffs. There are other athletic tappers out there. They are more covert. But the OSU Beavers are the most out there and open adherents.

EFT claims that it can be used to treat pretty much anything—anxiety, OCD, fears, eating disorders, allergies, weight loss, depression, ADD-ADHD, and everything this side of Alzheimer's and pancreatic cancer. Deepak endorses EFT, which is a New Age version of having Oprah pick your book. But despite this, Coach Stephen, who openly admits to being a clever marketer, decided that a method whose Web site depicts the earth with a dove flying around it was not going to be a big seller with the fellas. Hence, Renegade Mindset.

We tap the points under my collarbone several times. I can't say that I'm feeling generally cleared. I'm feeling generally dubious.

Then all hell breaks loose. Stephen asks me what I want to focus on during my tapping session. Is there a golf-specific phobia or issue that I'm having? Is there a nongolf problem that I want to get rid of or clear out and improve my game as a by-product?

I am a cautious man by nature. I don't like to tell people about my problems, even if I'm writing a book about them. I have spent therapy sessions talking about the White Sox bullpen. When I am asked how I'm doing, I almost always say "good." I never say, "anxious," or "not so good."

Yet, somehow, sitting there with a bald man in front of me and another bald one behind me, I decide to let go. I open up completely and begin telling Stephen (and Bill) that I have made strides with my anxiety, but that it is ultimately the biggest problem in my life. Yes, I've tried therapy. Yes, I've tried medication. I am doing pretty well. But, I tell them, I want it totally gone. I don't want to be scared to go to the dentist because I fear that I have oral cancer. I don't want to wonder at some point each day how much time I have left. I don't want to be aware of my own mortality—which I so keenly am every day of my goddamn life. I want to be free, damn it. I want that emotional freedom.

All right then.

We decide to access this through visualizing my golf game. I am asked to imagine a moment on the course that causes me anxiety. I volunteer a long downhill putt. Coach Stephen wants me to feel every emotional aspect of that kind of shot. What are both the physical and mental sensations that I experience? How do they rank on a scale of 1 to 10?

Sitting there I come to a realization that I am pretty much always a 5 or 6 on the anxiety scale. Most days, I just try to blow right past it, but even when there is no specific reason or trigger, I am pretty much feeling like something is gaining on me and that disaster is inevitable.

I visualize the putt. The imaginary green in my head is the fourth hole at my home course, and the entire scene is very dark, with a downhill putt from the back that breaks both ways to a pin set near the front. It is a chilling vision. Then we tap, focusing on the negative.

Here's how it works. You tap with two fingers several times on the following points in the following order:

1. the inside edge of your eyebrow
2. the outside corner of your eye socket
3. under your eye
4. one finger on your upper lip, the other between your chin and lower lip
5. one hand flat on the pit in your chest
6. your wrists together
7. the top of your head.

Throughout all of this, I mention negative emotions with each tap: anxious, anxious, anxious; worried, worried, worried.

When I am done, I breathe in once deeply through my nose and then blow it out my mouth.

We do this exercise several times.

I am again asked to imagine the putt. Inside of my head, I am putting from the dark into the light. Despite my misgivings, I am feeling more relaxed. A 2 rather than a 6. When I hit the putt, I stroke it nicely and it usually drops. I am flabbergasted.

But, this isn't enough for me, nor is it enough for Coach Stephen. We are going for emotional freedom—and emotional freedom we will have. So, we "scratch the record," which means that we alternate a positive affirmation with a negative one as we tap. Relaxed, relaxed (tap the eyebrow); anxious, anxious (tap the outer corner of the eye); and so on.

When we go back to the imaginary putting, the ball has become a streak of light. I actually begin trying to miss, but no matter what I do, I simply can't miss—as if there were a strong force at the bottom of the imaginary hole using gravitational pull to draw the ball right in.

We are not done, however. It is time, Coach Stephen says, to go after the big dog. And despite the laser-beam can't-miss putts I was making in my head, I remain very, very skeptical. Looking back, I now realize that one of my most firmly held beliefs is that I will always be anxious—which is the big dog of which Coach Stephen speaks.

He asks where I carry that anxiety and I say, "In my chest." We do some EFT and the anxiety level continues to drop from where the putting exercise left off—it is now very low, maybe a .5. But, as is often the case, Coach Stephen tells me—when the anxiety recedes, fears arise.

"I know this sounds New Agey and it makes me want to throw up," Coach Stephen says, "but what would your anger say if it could talk?"

I feel somewhat dumbfounded to answer this question and begin launching into a digressive ramble about the conflicts inherent in modern American manhood—that we are supposed to be simultaneously relaxed and also be high achievers. I am going nowhere and stalling for time. Coach Stephen looks at me, smiles, and says, "Help me, Josh, help you."

I default to my Therapy 101 answer of "I probably really hate myself; thus I send these hateful messages to myself all the time to remind me of what a fuckup I am."

We take this right to the EFT. I start tapping while I say, "I accept that I don't accept myself." Then we start scratching the record by adding, "Even though I am imperfect, I accept myself." This is followed by, "I am not perfect, even though I should be," then, "But I accept myself, or I will consider accepting myself."

When we are done, I tell Coach Stephen that I am not sure I am conquering my fears—that I feel blurry. He tells me that oftentimes when we are stuck in one belief system and exiting into another, there is fog at the doorway to choosing. I am in that fog, circling the O'Hare airport of happiness, I guess.

Thus, the pursuit of the big dog continues as Bill takes over.

My brain, he tells me, doesn't know the difference between what I vividly imagine and reality. What he then asks me to imagine is my anxiety—residing in my chest, causing my heartburn, causing my bloated stomach, and all resulting from the big dog itself, fear.

I am told to imagine my anxiety as a wheel inside of my chest and stomach, forever pushing the fear down and around, never leaving. I follow his direction and see a Technicolor circle that spins and spins. He then tells me to spin it backwards, reversing the field—and making it spin upwards instead of down.

As if I were Jack Nicholson in *The Witches of Eastwick* cherry-puking scene, I let out a horrific burp that emits acid and gas through my mouth. This happens several times. Bill tells me that it will take me twenty-one to thirty days to change a habitual pattern like my anxiety, and we head to the driving range.

o o o o

We arrive at a big suburban golf bubble, where Coach Stephen asks me to putt from various places with and without tapping. It is not Coach Stephen's fault, but I am feeling gigantically self-conscious; thus it's hard to discern the difference. The same happens when Bill and I go over to the mats and I try to crank out a bunch of 6-irons. As he talks to me, I keep looking at the other guys who have chosen to spend a weekday afternoon hitting balls into a soft white dome, wondering if they know what I'm doing—and assuming that they actually care why I have two guys telling me what to do. My swing becomes less free. I get more and more tense. I really like these guys, but I am overloaded. I want to go home.

Bill then asks me to imagine something that makes me really, really angry. I begin to picture an argument I had with some neighbors a while back. We take that experience, slow it down, rewind it, and draw Mickey Mouse ears and other silly stuff on the neighbors, and then speed it up to a Keystone Cops pace. Now I really want to go home.

This is not Bill's fault; nor is it Coach Stephen's. I am simply overwhelmed by the fact that I haven't found "the cure." That there is no magic pill. That I will not go back to Chicago and be able to say, "It's over; I'm OK." On some level that has been my hope. Instead, I now realize that all of this will be a lot of work.

Sitting at the Columbus Airport, I remember that one of the key elements of how to change my bad habits is willingness. There is the old saying, "The teacher will appear when the student is ready." Though I want more than anything to be ready, I am not sure that I am. I go through the entire day in my head. Wondering if it could really be this simple. If I can simply tap and imagine my problems away, or if it is far more complex. On the one hand, ever since I saw Yellin I have been a big believer that no matter how good or bad my swing, I need to trust that it is good enough every time that I get on the course. That the best thing we can do is to let go of results, both on the course and in our emotional life. Yet, that is exactly the problem that I now face. I am more convinced that no matter what I learn, I will always default to the anxiety. That the only cure is to really get out of my own way and walk through that fog and open the door to finding my authentic swing and learn how to trust it. To trust that everything is okay. And most of all to trust myself. That is my compliance issue. My road to nirvana, I now see, will not be a simple one.

Enter the Sensei

One does not need buildings, money, power, or status
to practice the Art of Peace. Heaven is right where you are
standing, and that is the place to train.

—O Sensei

I discovered the Golf Sensei via her Web site for Kiai (pro-
nounced "key-eye") Golf. I had been looking for an integration
of golf and the martial arts, then found it in the perfect package: a
fifty-two-year-old woman (civilian name Jamie Zimron) with a
fifth degree black belt in Aikido, who was also a licensed psycho-
therapist and former Top-10 Junior who'd played at Stanford and
was an LPGA teaching professional. On top of that, she was an
olive-skinned, dark-haired, brown-eyed Milwaukee native who
could pretty much pass for my older sister.

A few weeks after seeing Coach Stephen, I boarded a plane to San Diego for three days with the Sensei. On my flight I read a book that I'd picked up at Borders after seeing *Horton Hears a Who* with my oldest son, William. It was by someone named Osho, who seemed to have nearly an entire shelf to himself in the spirituality section—all books with single word titles: *Freedom, Intimacy, Intuition,* and *Courage.* I purchased *Joy,* figuring that freedom, intimacy, intuition, and courage might flow more easily if I had walked the path to joy.

Now, I didn't know anything about Osho before picking up this book, and from a trip to his Web site I gathered that he was a now deceased Indian mystic and spiritual leader of some kind. It was only later that I would find out that he had proclaimed himself the "Rich Man's Guru" and decided to underscore that moniker by driving a different Rolls-Royce pretty much every day.

But Osho wasn't all about the bling. No guru is. Except Oprah. Instead, he was a man with something to say about the way we live; in short, dividing the world into two kinds of people: the asleep and the awake.

The sleepers are a depressing lot. Their only sustenance is sensation—and they are drawn to seeking momentary and ephemeral pleasures in the same way every American child above the age of two is drawn to the majestic golden arches of McDonald's. Sleepers essentially want to be titillated—as if sex, booze, and food are all that there is to life. Don't feel the need to raise your hand. I'm not raising mine. But, yeah, I'm that guy. Toss in an updated kitchen and maybe some crystal meth and you've pretty much captured the way most of us view life at some point, regardless of where we come from.

But the problem with these classic seekers of external stimulus is that their pleasure works for a short time; it is fleeting—and then they are back to suffering their suffering until they magically bounce into the next sensation.

By contrast, the awake folks have it going on. They can be sitting in the bowels of a Malaysian prison for decades, listening to *Yanni Live at the Acropolis*, but they are all good. That's how damn awake and how centered, happy, and able to surf life's waves these folks are. They've been to the mountaintop. They are way past pleasure. They are even past joy. Their day-to-day lives are a meditative example of living in a little something Osho calls "Bliss."

I long to be that awake, but also realize that every time I think that I've met or know someone who fits this description, they will—with frightening dependability—turn out to have some horrific secret life in which they beat their children, laugh at Jay Leno's monologue, or pray to L. Ron Hubbard. As if to demonstrate this fact, the minute I entered my hotel room in Carlsbad, I turned on CNN to a bit of surprising news about Governor Elliot Spitzer. Like I said, frightening dependability.

As always, however, there is a third category, which Osho claims is very small and which I believe is very large (or perhaps I just like company): those of us who are in between, a little bit awake, a little bit asleep, and a whole lot confused about what we are doing here—particularly when a season of *Mad Men* ends and we realize there is almost nothing worth watching for the next six months. We know that our sleeper side is pushing metaphysical water up a hill; we know that we can be better than we are and we want more than titillation—we want to be genuinely happy, with more birdies and fewer doubles. We know it's within us.

The problem is that—at least for me—the enlightenment comes like drips from an IV when what I really want is a spiritual version of the way Keith Richards must feel every year or so when he goes to get his blood filtered and changed.

Thus far on my journey I'd been able to pick up a thing or two from each of my teachers—just like those IV drips of enlightenment. I'd avoided total confusion and with each lesson began to understand a bit more of what I'd learned from those that I'd seen before. While I felt that I was on the right path towards a deeper understanding of golf and life, I also sensed that I was holding disparate strands that needed to be pulled together into something bigger than its parts. I needed to find something that would help me become whole. And this is when I visited the Sensei.

o o o o

The Sensei is intense, but not in an off-putting, Tom Cruise way. Instead, she is intense in a way that draws you in. It is an intensity borne of pretty much being fully present and enthusiastic about whatever she is doing and whomever she is with.

Sitting in the restaurant at the Encinitas Ranch Golf Club, where she teaches, we very quickly got into the nature of energy (*Ki*) and the way of Aikido. We were surrounded by retirees who were downing BLTs and Arnold Palmers before their 3 P.M. Wednesday league teed off—making it an unlikely venue, but if I could meditate with Doc Parent at the café, I could get into a philosophical discussion about what makes lettuce grow (hint: "energy") and the differences in the inherent life forces of an organic salad from Whole Foods and the one you get at Arby's.

But first we needed to talk about O Sensei. Because, though I hate to imagine it, there was once a world without a Golf Sensei. That, however, was by necessity, because before there could be a Golf Sensei, there needed to be Aikido and thus the need for its creator—O Sensei.

Now, O Sensei, whose real name is Morehei Ueshiba, doesn't disappoint. Pull him up on a Google image search. Thank me later. You will see a man who is round of head, pointy of beard (which is white as the driven snow), and searching of gaze. You will see a man who is straight from central casting for a powerful, potentially inscrutable, always wise, and definitely mysterious mystical martial artist–meets–Zen master. A man who could kill Jackie Chan with a sneeze.

O Sensei was tiny. About five feet tall. But he was a Shinto priest and a master of pretty much every martial art. He was a very powerful dude, yet, by the age of forty, was bored with nowhere to go—at least as it pertained to learning various ways to kick ass. And with his immense talent as a martial artist came big responsibility. Thus, O Sensei came to a realization—he didn't want to attack people anymore. Instead, like a Jedi, he would only fend off attacks. The greatest power, he reasoned, came from choosing peace. If O Sensei had been elected president in 2000, the Dow would likely be at 17,000 and there would be no federal budget deficit.

Changing his ways sent O Sensei on something of a peace and circus trick jag where he demonstrated the innate power in life energy by doing things like dodging bullets. Apparently he figured out that they all traveled at the same speed—all he needed to do was make sure he moved enough to get out of their line. And when he wanted to turn on the major league stuff he could—it is said—repel an assault by several martial artists of another stripe (the non-Aikido kind who apparently attack) by pretty much not moving, but instead turning their energy against them, which sent them flying through the air.

"True victory is self victory," the Golf Sensei told me, summing up O Sensei's purpose in creating Aikido. "There is no enemy out there. The only enemy is the mind of discord within."

She could have just as well said, "You have come to the right place."

Aikido breaks down like this:

Ai—unity, harmony.

Ki—energy, life force, Chi.

Do—Tao, a way of harmonizing and becoming one with the universe.

During the next three days, the Golf Sensei would teach me to use my life energy and to harmonize it with the energy of the universe, thus expanding my powers beyond those of my mind and body, which would hopefully help me access my intuitive mind and fulfill the potential that is my birthright. The goal: a unity of body, mind, spirit, and emotion that is like a symphony where everyone is playing together, rather than the Ted Nugent–meets–Yo-Yo Ma thing I've been working on for most of my life.

There will be obstacles, the biggest of which is that "The ego is what blocks off our access to our manifold powers."

o o o o

"What makes your ball go?" the Sensei asks me at lunch.

"Me?" I respond.

"Your life energy, that's what makes the ball go," she says.

Energy, if properly used, is what helps people spontaneously heal from cancer. It is what made the slow, weak, small Gretzky dominate larger, better athletes. It is how that fifty-five-year-old guy, who is 5′9″, 145, can hit the ball 270 yards, while your 6′2″, 210 pound, forty-one-year-old ass needs the planets to align to hit one 250. I buy it.

But there is a catch. You don't just go, "OK, life energy, I'm ready for you." You must go to it.

"What if we go [to our life energy] as the source of under-standing?" the Sensei asks.

I'm with her. The best decisions I've made have had little to do with my rational mind and everything to do with my intuitive, irrational, life-energy-fueled mind. Getting married. Having the fourth kid. Changing careers and becoming a writer. The house we couldn't afford—but bought anyway. Yes, it's also made some bad calls along these lines: the puppy (our third dog) who has spent the last two years eating dirty diapers and strewing them around the house; the third car for the Colombian nanny, who turned out to be undocumented without insurance or a valid license and was eventually fired for slapping one of my kids. Life energy has its downside, though I may be confusing it with whimsy and impracticality. But, overall, I think it's the way to go. I'll err on the side of intuition and life energy.

Golf, the Sensei tells me, is a "really great way to transform yourself and start to function as a whole, holistic human being."

Thus we head for the range where I am to learn "the mechanics for the magic."

o o o o

For ten minutes or so, I hit balls with my 7-iron. I wasn't connecting to much other than swing thoughts from Waldron, Doc Parent, Yellin, and others who were trying to teach me to banish swing thoughts. That said, I thought I was hitting the ball fairly well.

The Sensei stood a few feet away, black belt around her white golf skirt, an Aikido sword in her bag. She took pictures of me from several angles. She smiled. It was a nice smile. But also a smile that said, "Brother, you got a lot of work to do."

We looked at those pictures. They told a sad story. I was hunching over again. That was easily corrected. I also had a case of what is called "flying elbow," which really has no mystical elements. It was simple—if viewed from directly behind my back or the path of my backswing, I was holding my right elbow out at the top, like Joe Morgan, but without the pumping downward action, just hanging out there. I needed to keep it down at my side, almost pinned to my torso during the takeaway. Again, that wasn't so hard to get. Not terribly metaphysical.

There was something bigger missing. My swing was all effort. I was going after the ball, instead of putting all of my energy into my swing.

The Sensei told me to watch a stocky guy in his mid-twenties who was about 30 feet to my left, hitting balls.

"Look over there and watch," she said. "He's a big, strong boy just like you."

This is a great lead-in for explaining how much my swing sucked.

The big, strong boy was drilling it, but his swing was completely economical, effortless, and graceful. There was a flow, dare I say, a unified, relaxed connection to his life energy that he was probably unaware of, but was manifesting it through his golf swing.

"Where does your swing start?" The Sensei asked.

I stood there for a long time. Searching my brain for the right answer. For any logical answer. I was dumbfounded. After what seemed like a long time, I stammered Bob Newhart–style, "It . . . uh . . . well . . . um . . . I think it . . . with my right hand on the takeaway?"

Before she could respond, I changed my answer, "No, it's my left shoulder dipping."

"With your left instep," she said.

Okay. My instep. And this is where the learning began.

I was supposed to generate the backswing from my left instep, pushing downwards and inwards. I was supposed to generate the downswing from my right instep, pushing downwards and inwards.

I tried it. I felt like I was going to fall down. But I stuck with it. I tried to do nothing with my arms—to simply let them come along for the ride. The results—at first—were disastrous. I thought I might fall over at any moment. I feared I would miss the ball. I shanked. I clanked. And I . . . well, there's no other good word with "ank" in it, but I'd have done that too.

The Sensei pulled out the Aikido sword. She showed me how to grip it, with my hands forming a V down the center of the grip. In Aikido, the whole thing is about putting the energy—yours and that of the universe—into the point of the sword. Thus, the sword finds its mark and when it gets there, it's got lots of power. We swung the Aikido sword for quite some time. The Sensei looked great doing it. I imagine I looked exactly as stupid as I felt.

The theory here is that with our feet—the connection to the earth—we can pull up the energy of the universe through the legs, merge it with ours, and send it down through our arms, through the V in our grip, and into the clubhead via the shaft. Laugh all you want, but there is precedence for this in the two meisterworks in the golf-and-spirituality canon—*Golf in the Kingdom* and *The Legend of Bagger Vance*.

For Shivas Irons, it is something called "True Gravity," which is never defined, but Murphy nips around the edges. It is what Seamus MacDuff is working on in that cave of his. It is what allows Shivas to shoot his midnight hole-in-one on Lucifer's Rug with a shillelagh and a feathery ball.

"True gravity," Shivas tells Murphy, "'tis Seamus's term for the deeper lines o' force, the deeper structure of the universe. But, this is the thing . . . ye can only know wha' it is by livin' it yersel—not through squeezin' it and shovin' it the way they do at universities and laboratories. Ye must go into the heart o' it, through yer own body and senses and livin' experience, level after level right to the heart o' it. Ye see, Michael, merely shooting par is second best. Goin' for results like that leads men and cultures and entire worlds astray. But, if ye do it from the inside ye na' . . . Ye must start from the inside."

While you get your mind around that, there is also Shivas's concept of "feeling yer inner body," which he directs Murphy to do as they swing the shillelagh together producing a "growing power, rhythm, and grace—a pleasure that had no apparent cause."

If that is not enough for you, there is also the concept of "the field" in Bagger Vance.

"Around [Bobby] Jones, encompassing his body in vibrating concentric fields, spread an aurora of energy. It seemed to be his body, but expanded, augmented. It was a field in itself. Then there were other fields. An infinitude of them. You could see his will, as Bagger Vance said, his intention select the field he chose, which was the fairway and the target line. Lines of force which were chromatic not just visually but aurally as well, vibrating like music, extended from Jones's intentionality . . . the force lines seemed to exist outside time, independent of it . . . They seemed to exert an intentionality of their own."

I'm sure you're confused. But, the thing here is—and it's neither easy to understand nor do at first—this: 1) using your feet to generate the swing not only draws energy from the earth and its gravitational pull, but it also leaves your arms to the forces of gravity. They are not acting independently; they are acting in concert with a natural law. The mechanics and feel of this will be explained later. 2) Your inner body works in concert with this. In some ways this is like Osho's concept of being "awake." If you are asleep your existence all takes place on the surface, both literally and figuratively. You seek things that appeal to your basic senses. But beneath that is something more. Something richer. If you can tap into the things that rest beneath your skin and your senses of sight, smell, taste, and other conscious manifestations, you can get in touch with that intuitive feel that makes everything okay. Drawing the energy from the earth (if you don't buy it, just imagine you are drawing the energy from your feet or whatever works) upwards through your insides, not on your skin or just under it, and down into the head of the club allows you to tap into that inner body, where your best golfing self resides.

This may sound like a bunch of bullshit to you. It may seem like New Age crap. But, remember the times when you played your best golf. Now take away those times where you were waiting for the magic to dissipate—and for the birdies and pars to turn to bogeys. Just remember the times where you stepped up and hit your drive without thought and it went down the middle. Then you took out your 6-iron, lined up toward your target, stepped over the ball and put it on the green, where your putts seemed to ride on a laser beam that aimed directly at the hole—and it went on and on like that. Where golf seemed like a simple game. And remember the way it felt. I may be insane, or maybe I am too immersed in Murphy and Pressfield, but those moments have a vibration to them, they have a frequency; I am not living or playing on the surface; instead I am as close to my inner body as I've ever been—and somehow the contours of the course seem to merge with my body, my club, and my game. It's not a big mystical thing. But it's a feeling of well-being, not very unlike what Murphy describes above.

As best as I can tell, that is how you can define true gravity and the field.

o o o o

The Sensei and I worked for quite a while on this. I stood on two swiveling disks and moved my feet back and forth. I did a bunch of Aikido stretches that left me tired and sore. I put my club on my head with no intention of snapping it—instead, I was holding it with both hands and using my feet to simulate the swing. I did slow-motion drills using only my feet. I worked my ass off.

I was nowhere near mastery or understanding in that moment, but about one in ten shots was magical. In those moments my hands and arms did nothing of their own volition. Instead, they remained relaxed and soft as they floated up on the backswing automatically and did the same down through the ball. The feeling in those moments where I wasn't trying to use my arms and hands to make sure I hit the ball or to try to add extra force were nearly indescribable—my arms became like the wheels of a racecar, with my feet as the piston-pumping engine. The flight of the ball was remarkable. It was not just crisp and clean and straight, it was as if the ball had been shot from a cannon and was on a rail going directly where my eyes had intended. I was feeling and relaxing into my inner body—at least a tenth of the time.

o o o o

The following day we played at the LaCosta Resort and Spa, home base of Deepak Chopra. Sadly, I did not see the man himself, and I imagine he was bathing in a tub filled with rose petals, baby goat's milk, and thousand-dollar bills—as I'm guessing is his Wednesday custom.

The course at LaCosta is not unlike the one at Ojai Valley. It is impossibly green in that impossibly green way that is unique to certain parts of California. It is a green that doesn't exist in Chicago, Connecticut, or even Ireland. It is lush, warm, and screams something like "Dumbass, why don't you live in California?"

The Sensei and I played what I'll call an "experimental eighteen." I was very interested in results, but reminded myself that

I was integrating new material on every level and would grant myself time to adjust before I started the interior monologue about how much I suck.

There were some mulligans and second cracks at shots that didn't quite work out the way I'd hoped. It was your classic "playing lesson" with lots of on-course instruction. In fact there was enough teaching going on that I felt as if I might burst. The Sensei's ebullience bowled me over, while her "scratch-golfing big sister I never had" chemistry with me thwarted any desire I might have had to ask her to please stop.

I won't guess at my score. Instead, I look back and think there were ten or fifteen shots that I hit really well. Not like the one to three perfect shots a pro hits in a round, but still somehow qualitatively different from my usual ball striking. When I hit it well, a sense of warm well-being spread through my body. I don't claim it was a massive spiritual experience or awakening, but it bordered on that—or at least the sensation of having a small glass of really good whiskey or Scotch after coming in from the cold to sit before the fire. I felt unity with my club, the ball, and whatever energy the universe saw fit to send my way through the bottom of my spikes.

Most of all I recall a 220-yard, steep downhill shot from the rough on the right on a long, doglegged par-4, where my arms did almost nothing but channel energy—they were totally passive, but completely alive. My ball took off like a rocket, but then did something I hadn't done since I was a teenager—about 100 yards out, it seemed to catch a headwind that made it rise 15 or so feet while it continued towards the hole, then came down at exactly the right angle and location, sticking a foot from the cup, which was tucked into the left rear corner of a long, narrow green that offered death to anyone who was over. I tapped in for birdie.

o o o o

Our last day together we met at Arrowwood Golf Course and were paired up with a gentleman I will call Dewey. He was a nice enough old guy with the bearing of a retired mid-level military officer and a bug up his ass you couldn't kill with a howitzer. It wasn't his fault. He was just that way.

I saw a mild look of "Oh, great," when he realized he was playing with a woman. We then teed it up from the blues, the Sensei along with us. Now Dewey's look went the way of "Oh, brother, I can't wait to see this."

The Sensei then poked one deep down the middle. My drive was wide right and into some brambly gorseish stuff. Dewey's drive was struck with a swing that made your teeth hurt—filled as it was with tension, unspoken indeterminate rage, and a sense that if you hit the fucking thing hard enough it'd go a long way.

As we pressed on, Dewey only got tighter. To his credit, however, he fairly quickly got over the fact that he was playing with a woman. In fact, I sensed some admiration as she made flawless golf look somewhat routine.

My game was marked by high highs, and low lows. There were a few triples and several doubles. But, there were many pars and two birdies as I came in at 90. Two things stuck with me, however, and neither of them was my score.

First were pictures the Golf Sensei took of me during that round and the way in which they contrasted with those taken two days before on the range at Encinitas. I was no longer hunched over, and the flying elbow was gone. Another "before" photo showed my "posa" (Sensei talk for the way you look at the end of your swing) after a drive, in which I looked like a batter who'd taken a giant hack and stepped out of the box to either admire his homer or head back to the dugout. My left front foot was parallel to my right. It hardly even looked like golf.

There were also two pictures of my follow-through. In one I was coming out of a trap. In the other I had just hit my 2-hybrid off of the fairway. In each, I looked like a pro; my left foot was still horizontal, while I stood on the toes of my right. My stance was upright and my arms were fully extended but relaxed. The club was floating over my left shoulder. It wasn't quite Vijay, but it was close enough to be on a Titleist commercial.

Oh, and the other thing I remembered? The Sensei was 1 over playing from the blues.

o o o o

When I returned home I made an unexpected change in my lifestyle that had little to do with golf, though the trip to San Diego and the reading of Osho had been the only intervening variables. One morning after I dropped my two middle boys at school and headed to Starbucks for a cup of coffee, I decided to turn off sports radio for the first time in fifteen years. Maybe I suddenly saw the field, maybe not, but I realized that listening to people scream about events that I already knew about and that would change the next day was not helping me in any way. I was, to my surprise, actually becoming concerned about what my brain consumed.

I began either driving in silence or listening to NPR. *SportsCenter*, the Internet, and the *Chicago Tribune*, I realized, were sufficient for my sports information needs. Yes, I endured the never-ending daily debates about school reform, the inevitable story about Navajo blanket-weaving, and the NPR voice that seems to emanate from every single person who has ever broadcast on the public airwaves, that whole Carl Kassel–Robert Segal–Noah Adams tone that is borne of some off-the-beaten-path "more intellectual than the Ivys" school like the University of Chicago. Somehow it didn't bother me at all.

And damn if I didn't feel better. Less jangly. Better informed. More relaxed.

I spent thirty minutes each day up in my office doing drills that would keep me generating my swing from my feet and drawing peaceful power from the earth. I did them slow-motion in the mirror, as Waldron had done. I couldn't wait until the snow melted and I could get out, which I did a few weeks later at a scraggly, par-62 municipal course a few blocks from my house, where the sites include not only the famed Bahai Temple, but also the El tracks and a sanitary canal.

I was hitting it well. There were many growing pains. I wasn't seeing the field or feeling my inner body, but I felt some sense of true gravity on a few swings. As it was a warm, lovely spring day, there were a few people out on the course. After five holes, I ran into two guys in their mid-twenties waiting on the tee at a 290-yard par-4 where a long drive would inevitably hit the telephone or power wires.

"Sir, would you like to play through? We're pretty bad."

"Sure," I said, then I stepped up and launched a 230-yard 3-wood that was like a beautiful bullet down the middle.

"Great shot, sir," the other one said.

For the first time in my life it didn't dawn on me to say something like "Don't call me 'sir'; my name is Josh."

Instead, I picked up my bag and said, "Enjoy yourselves, boys. And thanks."

CHAPTER
8

A Swing Is Reborn

Only one golfer in a thousand grips it lightly enough.

–Johnny Miller

SUMMER 2008. STOCKBRIDGE, MASSACHUSETTS

As I walked up from the parking lot at Kripalu, I saw a large expanse of lawn where four women sat far apart from each other. Two were meditating. One was talking softly on her cell phone. The fourth, a purple-clad yogini, was clutching a soy-based water bottle and crying. As I walked closer to the front door (which bears the words: "exploring the yoga of life") I felt like crying myself.

Before I could reach the front door, however, I needed to get past two young men on the stairway who looked like refugees from the casting call for an *Into the Wild* sequel. One of these bearded spiritual layabouts was playing guitar in the manner in which all such young men play guitar, emitting nonspecific folksy tunes that create a subtle threat that at any moment he will break into a rendition of "Needle and the Damage Done." The other, in some moment of reverie, inspired no doubt by the glorious day that God had given us, spontaneously launched himself upside down into a yoga handstand. If this pair had their own biblical plague, Hacky Sack balls would rain from the sky, and the rivers would turn to soy milk.

Resisting the impulse to break the guitar or push the now inverted deadbeat over, I politely made my way inside the former monastery that now houses Jon Kabbat Zinn's Buddhistish retreat in western Massachusetts. I went to the front desk, grabbed my recyclable name tag, and was shown to my room—a spare but clean place with a bathroom, a bed, two small night tables, and a ceiling fan. From my window, there was a view of the lovely and serene Monk's Lake.

Yes, I thought, this is what I signed up for: this part of my quest towards emotional, spiritual, and golf enlightenment. But, frankly, I felt as though I was at the worst sleepover camp in the world.

o o o o

Dinner is a buffet consisting of quinoa corn cakes and a bunch of mushy, vegetarian-macrobiotic-vegan crap. That said, the spelt-kamut bread isn't bad and I discover a decent goat cheese and pecan salad. Never in my entire life, I have to say, have I actually been relieved to find a tasty salad.

This is a big part of my challenge. I must accept that for sixty or so hours, food is simply food. For my wife this would be easy. If she were here she'd say, "It's just fuel. Every meal doesn't have to be some kind of sublime victory that satisfies you in ways that normal human contact could never hope to achieve."

As you may have gathered, my wife isn't Jewish. Because, for me—and frankly most other Jews—food is pretty much the reason we showed up for this big party called life. And for people like us, this buffet is a crisis. No Chinese. No Italian. Every meal just fulfilling some kind of biological purpose and having no significant payoff other than that it keeps you moving forwards and alive.

Munching on the dusty corncakes, I look around the room and take in the primarily female crowd, which is made up mostly of cute young yoga instructors and middle-aged women who look like they either a) have crawled out of those *New Yorker* cartoons of the fuzzy people or b) own feminist bookstores in communities where they and their friends are the only feminists.

There are a few couples, all of whom look surprisingly, intensely, overwhelmingly into each other's eyes in that way that screams: "THIS WEEKEND IS THE LAST CHANCE WE HAVE TO SAVE OUR MARRIAGE."

o o o o

At 7:30 we convene in the Sunset room. As I enter, I am reminded to take off my shoes by the bearded guy with the guitar.

"Hey," he says, as I walk past him, "Mats Sundin." And then begins humming and whistling some tune that I've never heard.

Then I remember that I'm wearing a Toronto Maple Leafs shirt. Reflexively I respond, "Börje Salming," a legendary Toronto defenseman of my childhood. If I'd really had it together I would have invoked the name of legendary Leafs coach Punch Imlach, but dinner had left me out of sorts.

"Awesome," he says.

I decide then and there that I kind of like this guy. Perhaps I'd judged him too quickly. The common parlance of sports will do that for you. Thus, if I am forced to kill everyone at Kripalu this weekend, I will either spare him or, when his time comes, be as merciful as possible about the method of his demise.

o o o o

I have not seen a photograph of Les Bolland's aura, nor have I examined his chakras. But, I can assure you that he is made up of a very, very pure version of what the New Age folks like to call "energy." Now, this doesn't simply mean that he is energetic. Instead, it means that, even though we are all made up of energy, his energy is front and center. That energy is who he is in many ways. It reverberates when you meet him or even when the two of you are in the same room.

Tan, trim, and in his mid-fifties, Bolland is a Floridian, by way of Liverpool, who looks a decade younger and hasn't a gray strand of hair on his head as far as I can tell. True, he has no kids, which seems to help in this department, but I also ascribe it to his macrobiotic diet, genetics, and well, to that energy that he emits.

"Most people don't play golf," he tells the ten or so of us gathered for his clinic at Kripalu. "They work golf."

In this group, there are some veterans, myself included, who know what it is to work golf. The group, however, is an interesting mix. There are some who have never hit a ball. There are a few who are there because they like to come to Kripalu. There is a husband and wife. And then there is a man whom I will call Ira, a dyspeptic, psoriasis-ridden, potbellied retired businessman from Jersey who started playing golf last summer (I imagine someone told him it was relaxing) and is now beset with an endless string of mind-numbing instructions that rattle through his head when he works the game. Barely ten minutes into the clinic he has mentioned the need to keep one body part at 80 degrees and another at 90.

"You've got an advantage," Les says to Ira. "You've got no experience."

Les begins telling us that to achieve peace and harmony while expressing our true swings, we need to get rid of such mind-chatter. Having this large instructional pole up our collective golfing asses, Les says, is the single biggest factor that prevents us from playing the game well.

"Once you tell your body what to do, you become restricted," he says, with nods of agreement all around.

Tour pros, we are told, are primarily guys who took up the game before the age of eight. That is the key age, Les claims, at which our intellect kicks in and starts judging and commenting on what we do. Most pros learned without the interference of the conscious mind, by trial and error—an organic process that lets them find their own swings without remembering to keep the left arm straight and the head down. Their games are about responding and making things up as they go along. By having developed a swing that simply felt good—and worked—they are miles ahead of the rest of us mentally. When asked to explain their swings, Les claims, most pros will simply say "I have no idea." It's why they seldom write great instructional books, but it's also why they can go out and decimate Pebble Beach for four consecutive rounds.

"The fundamental swing is a feeling. It's not a concept," he says. "The goal is not to understand it. The goal is to do it."

For the pros, golf is as natural as walking. Which is how we get to a discussion of how we learn to walk and how you would explain how to walk to someone. As one of us tries to break down the walking process piece by piece, Les begins walking around like a stiff-legged Frankenstein, to illustrate how one might walk if they were thinking about how to walk: "I pick this foot up and then put it down. . . . "

In truth we learn to walk by trial and error. We fall a lot. We fall forward. We fall backward. We fall to the side. We walk really fast and we walk really slow. What we are doing, Les says, is toying with the extremes of our ability to balance ourselves and move our bodies. That is what we must do with our swings. And this weekend, the ten of us will relearn our swing and find the natural flow to be reborn as the golfers we can truly be. We are here to find our swings, something like the authentic swing, but Les's work is more informed by Ernest Jones's *Swing the Clubhead* and Tim Galwey's *The Inner Game of Golf* than by Bagger Vance.

"This is all about giving up control," Les tells us.

It is over-controlling that brings us pain on the course—and in our lives. I added the part about our lives, but it's true. Attempts to control the outcome of any event—your golf score, your kid's life, your career—usually end up putting your mind in a place it shouldn't be: the future. The Buddha and his peeps call this grasping or striving. It is one of the two primary forms of suffering, along with the desire to push away bad things and disavow them. The sufferer is one who tries to get rid of the bad in life and has a ton of energy invested in ensuring that only good befalls him or her.

To Les, the desire to control is perhaps the single biggest obstacle to playing good golf. Like marijuana, it is a gateway drug that leads to all kinds of other problems, which stem from the inordinate amount of respect we show for the ball and the course. We should respect neither, Les says.

A perfect example of how this happens can be demonstrated by the natural tendency of most golfers with a handicap over 5 or so to push, slice, or fade the ball. There are legions of us out there who aim a few feet left of every target as a compensation. The great golfers, according to Les's friend Dennis, a gentle-natured local pro, have the opposite problem at some point in their careers—they tend to hook. It was Hogan's natural hook that put him on the path to discovering "the secret," which some claim is meaningless primarily because it relates to hooking—and those of us who need help couldn't hook it if we tried.

The fade/slice/push phenomenon, Les claims, is the result of being conscious of impact. We know the ball is there. Our goal is to hit the ball, not to swing the club. And this is why we are all holding up momentarily, wanting to make sure that we are making contact, which leaves us flying out to the right instead of releasing our hands through as the pros do.

To illustrate this, Les asks one attendee to hold out his hand, and punches it. This is how we swing. Then he has the man hold out his hand again, and slaps it. That is the golf swing. It is a slap. A long, constant motion where the ball just happens to be in the way. We are here to be converted from punchers to slappers.

How do we do this? Well, the first step is to swing.

Les has all of us get centered in our *hara* or *tan t'ien* (also *dan tien*), which is located just beneath the navel. It is the place from which we derive balance—and in the Eastern spiritual world it is the core and center of our being. It is where our power comes from in just about everything from Pilates to ch'i kung (qigong). It is also the location from which we find peace and calm.

Finding my hara here at Kripalu, or anywhere else, has always been problematic. Throughout the weekend Les will admonish me to "sit in my belly" longer. I'm not sure how he can see that I am not sitting in my belly, but he does and he is right. At one point Dennis comes over and tries to help me find my center. He tells me that I should find the point where my tailbone tilts slightly forward when I am standing at address. Neither of them, however, is privy to the fact that I suffer from acid reflux and take Nexium to control my heartburn. A psychologist once told me that the stomach houses the most nerve endings of any location in the body and is what suffers most when we are anxious. Hence the Nexium and difficulty connecting to my hara.

No matter the condition of my tan t'ien, however, I find the swinging component freeing. We swing our arms back and forth as loosely as we can. Les implores us to "get sloppy." We can never get sloppy enough, he claims. If we think we are out of control, we might be sloppy at best. If we think we are sloppy, we are probably somewhat relaxed. If we think we're relaxed, we are in reality probably as laid back as Laura Bush on a trip to Zimbabwe.

So, to counter this we swing wildly, playing with the extremes, letting our arms, and the centrifugal force created by swinging them, take us where they will. We are doing this just to see what it feels like to swing with no purpose at all. The journey with no goal, a stark contrast from the way we perceive life as we stand on the first tee.

If any of us weren't becoming sufficiently loose from this exercise, Les counters it with a bit of shiatsu massage. Because I am an exalted member of the media, I assume that Les will give me a massage and then I can observe the others when it would have been my turn to do so. I am half right.

Les gives me an intense shoulder massage for a few minutes and then we switch and I am asked to rub the back of a young guy who works at Kripalu and is auditing the course. Immediately I get the creeping sense of inhibition that has plagued me my entire life. Everyone, I believe, is watching me. Everyone, I suspect, will think I'm weird—and frankly, gay—at least that's my delusion. I believe that qualifies my emotional age as somewhere around fourteen.

But I calm myself and massage this guy. I pretend nobody exists and just do—instead of thinking. The result is twofold. First, I massage this guy so hard that he keeps falling over forwards. But, second, I lose my inhibitions because I have no choice but to relax and give a male stranger a massage in front of other people—none of whom are paying attention anyway.

The purpose of this exercise, I believe, was to loosen us up both physically and mentally. To "shock the brain," as Les says, by taking us out of our comfort zone and unmooring us from our own suffering. It is very relaxing and freeing on every level. Or maybe I just liked rubbing this guy's back.

A few minutes later we pick up some sawed-off 3-irons with very heavy heads. Everyone is swinging much more freely. We are momentarily out of that place where we are swinging as we've been taught and are simply swinging for no good reason but to swing and to feel what it is to go fast and slow, up and down, over and over, not caring where the club goes.

"You can't grip it loosely enough," Les calls out during this exercise. "Hold the club as if it's about to fly out of your hands."

o o o o

Les knows a bit about trying to give up control. He took up the game at age ten, therefore not experiencing that magical time where he wasn't judging his own actions. He was "working" golf instead of playing it. But his level of working golf was good enough to get him on the European Tour and into the 1974 British Open, where he finished seventy-eighth. A dream for any of us out there hacking Bandon Dunes for $400 or simply playing the local muni. For Les, however, it was a nightmare.

"I was as tight as could be," he told me some months before the clinic. "I had no quality of the moment. No feeling. No enjoyment. I've never had a student—even my German students—who was as tight as I was."

Each year he got worse. Each year he made less money. And eventually he flamed out and quit the tour in late 1977. Then several things happened. In desperation to save his game he read every book he could on golf, including *Swing the Clubhead*.

"It was like a light bulb going off. The very idea to swing a weight on a piece of string was so new to me; for the first time in my life I actually felt something as a golfer. I was so over-controlled," he says. "There's no student I can't help open up, because I've done it myself."

Bolland moved to Germany and taught there, while also adopting a macrobiotic diet and taking up both yoga and shiatsu.

Those disciplines, mixed with the Ernest Jones classic and Galwey's book, became the essential elements of his teaching philosophy—which rests on the motto "Non Credo" ("Don't Believe").

Thus he asks us, why do we use so many clubs? Do we need several different wedges? Do we need to wear gloves? Do we need to use an interlocking grip?

In the spirit of the weekend I decide to abandon the glove and start swinging with a modified baseball grip where my thumbs point straight down the club, but without overlapping my fingers. The former makes me feel more in touch with the club and the latter loosens my grip considerably. Before I head home I adopt both permanently.

o o o o

By 9:30 everyone is exhausted, but we now know where the swing starts. Not with our feet, or in our mind, or our left knee. Instead, the clubhead is what moves us. We do not move it. And by following the motion of the clubhead and "letting the tool do the work" we are transformed. We begin to swing and take the first steps towards no longer playing golf. From this day forward, Les tells us, we are heading out to play swing.

o o o o

Day two begins with breakfast, where I am joined by a fellow clinic attendee. We are both eating oatmeal covered in natural maple syrup and talking about the previous day's activities. My new friend says that he is worried about losing the swing that made him a 15-handicap before he came to Kripalu. I assure him that he can always go back to it, but to just view the clinic as an experiment, and am surprised to realize that my mind is that damn open.

At 9:40 I am back in the Sunset room and rubbing another man's ass with my foot. Ira, the grumpy retiree who looks like a refugee from a 1970s Alka Seltzer commercial, is lying face down and I have been instructed to move him backwards and forwards with my foot, while concentrating on the center of his body, thus impacting his hara. I am told to put my foot on the small of his back, then his belt line—and then—yes, his ass. Again, I try to get uninhibited and relax into doing this work.

"Ow!!" Ira shrieks. "Jesus Christ!!"

"That's too hard, right?" I ask.

Before he can respond, Les has us walk on our partner's hands and fingers with our bare feet. I have repressed all memories of that experience.

But the hands are important. They are our point of contact with the club. We stretch and massage our own fingers, then hands, wrists, forearms, and biceps—moving away from the club. We do this to ourselves, massaging each area and trying to really feel it.

When we are done, Les explains that most swings are based on leverage. We are not going to follow that model. Instead, we are looking for centrifugal force. We want to feel the clubhead. It should be as if blood is flying into our fingertips from our arms as we swing, with the motion of the club carrying us.

Next we walk down to a soccer field with shag bags where we try to simply swing. It is a remarkable exercise in realizing how difficult it is to let go.

No matter how hard I try to simply just swing, my intellect and my body are in a death match. I am consumed with making contact. Occasionally I do let go. The result is either magnificently well struck—or well slapped—or I hit a foot behind the ball.

"Hitting and swinging are opposites," Les says. "Let's swing. Let the clubhead overtake you and do everything."

He walks over to where I am hitting and I do my best to really let it all hang out.

"You've got real talent, Josh," he tells me. "But, you've got to sit in your belly more."

I am amazed that I remember that second part. Because, in truth, the moment he told me I had "real talent" I became like all those soldiers in *The Manchurian Candidate*. I now will do anything Les Bolland tells me.

With the warm glow of that compliment in my head, I remember something that I'd been doing recently for anxiety, which had worked tremendously well. It's kind of like lying to myself, or actually more like telling the truth. What I do when I have a fear, say that I have cancer in my nose (yes, I had that fear) or that my acid reflux truly is evidence of a "more serious condition," I tell myself that the absolute opposite is true. It is a sad commentary on my thought processes, but the results have been nothing short of remarkable.

I decide to apply this to my swing. For weeks I've been trying to replicate what the Golf Sensei taught me. I have spent hours in my office and on the range trying to generate my swing completely with my feet and lower body. When it works, it's amazing. But when it doesn't, it's horrific and frustrating.

But, as the Sensei told me, the point of learning the kata (a Japanese word signifying the forms one practices in martial arts training) is to give up the kata. I can always go back to it, I tell myself. And thus, I just swing and, in doing so, am able to let myself be swung. Though there are duffs, I ignore them. I focus on the good shots. Holding the feeling of a good swing.

Les calls us over to a bunch of folding chairs. "Don't expect perfect. This is not a science. It's an art," he says. "Expect good swings. Not good shots."

A big, unathletic guy in his mid-sixties, who has never played golf in his life and has a laundry list of injuries from biking and motorcycle accidents, is asked to get up and hit a few. Standing calmly over the ball, he smoothly strokes a gorgeous 5-iron out about 160. I nearly crap my pants.

"We improve, not because of time," Les says. "We improve because of attitude."

About five minutes later I am giving this big guy a chair massage. "That's my bad shoulder," he says, wincing. "There's no collarbone there."

o o o o

At lunch I am treated to some kale-infused ground turkey on the "build your own burrito" bar. The sour cream appears to be real. The Vegenaise, however, resembles nothing I've ever put in my body.

I sit down at a table of strangers and listen to two men a few seats down having the following conversation.

"So, when I'm at work, sometimes I'll know that I have a call coming and it'll take me totally out of myself," says the one in the hipster glasses he's too old to be wearing.

"I know, it removes you from the moment," says his friend, who is similarly too old for his ponytail. "No matter what I do, I can't completely absorb myself in what I'm doing. I get out of my body and into my head. All because of the anticipation of a phone call."

I try to expand my heart in this moment . . . and fail miserably.

o o o o

In the afternoon we head out to a nice Ross-designed nine-hole course and bring only our 5-irons. We break into three groups and Les has me tee off first.

"And remember, Josh, don't embarrass yourself!!" he jokes.

I stand up at the tee, believing in my heart that I am the best golfer at this clinic not named Les or Dennis. After all, I have "real talent." I am also pretty sure that I am totally relaxed and have tossed away my old swing for a free and easy method where the club swings me.

Teeing it up, I address the ball and promptly hit about 9 inches behind my Callaway—the one that gives me softer feel on those tricky shots golfers like myself so often face—and make no contact with a shot for the first time in about fifteen years. And I was still drinking when I played in those days.

Somehow I'm not embarrassed, though I pretty much revert to my old swing when I re-tee and lace one about 180 down the right side.

The experiment in playing with only a 5-iron is interesting. On two, a long par-3, I'm the only one to reach the green from the tee. But, it's the old swing again. Same off the tee on three. Long, a bit to the right, and hit by someone completely aware of impact.

Then I hit my second shot on the third, an approach from 200 or so. "That's a swing!!" Dennis calls out the moment I hit it. And it felt great. I was totally relaxed and my body operated like a very mellow timepiece, with each cog hitting each gear just where it's supposed to. I suspect that it's the longest, smoothest stroke (with the most intensely coiled backswing) I've hit since my teens. The ball went straight as an arrow and just flew and flew—landing a bit short of the green.

For the rest of the day I completely detach from results. We are playing best-ball, so we all drop wherever the best shot landed. My "swings" are remarkably fluid. I don't care when I duff or push one.

I have no respect for the ball or the course. My ego is out of the way. And I'm not even playing golf anymore, I'm playing swing. Most importantly, I'm playing.

o o o o

The next morning something had come over me. I was completely at peace with eating the breakfast at Kripalu, and doing so in silence seemed almost a relief, not only because I didn't need to listen to any more neutered idiots who never played Little League (or if they did, I am glad I wasn't there) prattle on about how present they were or weren't at a piano recital or where they buried the placenta after little Journey was born, but also because I realized that it had probably been seven years since I'd had a quiet meal in my own home.

Matter of fact, the quinoa-based cream of wheat tasted pretty good drenched in the organic maple syrup.

o o o o

As the golfing portion of day three dawned, I realized that Ira was gone. In fact, I'm not even sure if he played in the 5-iron best-ball. I think he pretty much realized that he wasn't going to become a reborn golfer and got sick of the food and the whole vibe at Kripalu. Or perhaps he feared that the next man-on-man massage would involve scented oil and happy endings. Whatever the case, he was nowhere to be found.

The morning was an extension of the previous day. We worked on freeing up our swing. We swung and swung. We also watched a video of a four-year-old girl attempting to hit a golf ball. She hit it on top, she missed it, she knocked it backwards, and she made some decent contact once or twice. The video was to show us someone unencumbered by results, expectations, and mind chatter. To see someone in their natural state at play with a golf club in their hands.

I immediately started thinking of my five-year old son, Leo, whom I'd taken to the driving range on a few occasions. As I let him stand in the next stall, I couldn't resist suggesting that he look at the ball, stand properly, and follow through. I was a nightmare. I could see his ears turning red and he finally said, "Dad, leave me alone," after which he promptly hit the five-year-old equivalent of a good shot.

After the video we went down to the soccer field and Les had me swing in front of everyone. I was like a metronome, smoothly letting the clubhead take me through the proper motions and hitting some beautiful wedges—one after another. I was using less energy and the ball was flying further and straighter. My grip pressure was a 3 on a scale of 10. The club felt as if it was about to fly from my hands, but it didn't. Instead, it always found a way to get square and in the right position for impact—of which I was no longer conscious. I resolved that from then on, my only goals would be those that Les had laid out for me: "Does it feel good?" and "Did the ball fly?"

I was determined to play swing and let the chips fall where they may. For the first time I suspected I was finding my authentic swing.

o o o o

After playing nine holes in the afternoon—this time we could bring a hybrid, a wedge, and a putter as well—I went to hear a lecture by a man named Genpo Roshi entitled "Big Mind, Big Heart."

Gathered in the Sunset room were probably sixty or so Kripaluans. The Genpo, who is probably in his mid-sixties, came out and told us that he really never had a plan for such lectures. He asked if we had any questions, or where we'd like to start. Someone asked a question and then he launched directly into executing what I believe was a precisely fine-tuned lecture that he gives on all such occasions.

The basic idea was this. The human being is divided into two sections—the human and the being. The being is the totally together, neutral-minded self who is simply present. The human—for lack of a better way of putting it—is the rest of our shit. Genpo Roshi asked us to describe some of the aspects of the "human" side of things. I'm not sure who said it, but the first element was "the boaster," that part of us that likes to conflate our achievements and scream them from the hilltops. The audience, for a moment, was asked to play the part of "the boaster."

"Who are you?" Genpo Roshi asked us.

"The Boaster" we replied in unison.

Then people randomly called out boasts. "I am the smartest person in the room," said an Indian man. "My kids are better than your kids," a woman said.

The whole thing got quite crazy from there. We talked about "the Asshole." We divided that aspect of self into two parts—the immature and unproductive asshole, and the mature and productive asshole. The latter being the one who says, "Stop being such an asshole" to someone who is being the former.

As this went on, I mostly marveled at the alacrity with which members of the audience were able to immediately embody and assume the viewpoint of some mind state. I felt as if I was slow on the Zen uptake and that everyone else might just be a lot more together and evolved than I was.

Then, and I'm not sure how we got there, Genpo Roshi asked us to be "the Unborn." As my mind was still getting around this concept and everyone was responding "the Unborn" to the Genpo's "Who are you?" people quickly began offering opinions and feelings and statements from the viewpoint of the unborn. It was at this moment that I realized most everyone else in the room was out of their fucking mind.

At some point there was a misunderstanding between the side of the room acting as the "human" side and a woman who was on the "being" side. Her feelings seemed somehow rankled and before long she told everyone, in very genuine terms, that she had actually found inner peace. She said that she'd been through years of therapy, tried all kinds of different religions, and practiced everything from yoga and tai chi to having had her energy cleared and her chakras aligned. But she said that in the end, she had found inner peace when she decided to stop seeking, to give up the journey towards happiness and enlightenment and simply be. And that is when she found herself—right there, wherever she was.

It was a remarkably real moment to which most others in the room seemed completely oblivious—as they were probably figuring out how to best convey the messages processed by the mature, productive, unborn asshole—whoever that may be. The woman was near tears and I believed every damn word she said. I was deeply moved myself. I had no idea how I might get there, but I decided that it was time for me to set my golf game free. It was time to take a break from the lessons and venture forth into playing a few rounds with various clergymen, monks, and other golfing mystics and mystics who golfed, in hopes of finally finding that Shivas Irons with whom I could ascend to golfing and personal nirvana.

As I drove to the Albany airport the following morning, I called my wife and told her about the Genpo's lecture and the fact that I'd googled him later that evening and found out that his real name was Dennis Merzel and he was born in Brooklyn.

"You ever think that maybe you Jews ought to stick to your own religion?" my wife asked.

She was right. It was time to play golf with a rabbi.

Part Two

IN

Have the Jews Not Suffered Enough?

*Certainly there was no chance of me not believing in God—not after
a 390-yard tee shot with a persimmon driver.*

—Deceased golf pro Herman Fins-Winston, the protagonist
of Roland Merullo's Golfing with God

SUMMER 2008. CHICAGO, ILLINOIS / SAN FRANCISCO, CALIFORNIA

Upon returning from Kripalu, I decided to undertake an experiment. On a cold, blustery April day, I headed out to Willow Hill
Golf Course, a tricky nine-hole links layout that sits atop what
was once a garbage dump in Glenview, Illinois. My plan was to
have no plan other than using my 5-iron for nearly every shot
and to not keep score.

I had broached the topic of not keeping score with my father
at a Mother's Day brunch the preceding weekend. My dad is an
atypical seventy-two-year-old retired businessman, in that he is
currently teaching Pilates to Parkinson's patients and recently
received his Master's degree in Spanish literature. As you might

gather, for a man his age—or any age—he's a pretty nontraditional, open-minded guy.

When I get back from each trip he always wants to know whom I saw, what we did, and what I learned so that he can apply it to his own game. When I told him about Yellin's method for getting in the zone, he was all over it. When I explained the Golf Sensei's theory of drawing the peaceful power from the earth through your feet and legs, then running it down your arms into the club, he didn't bat an eyelash and went right out to the range and gave it a try. The idea of not keeping score, however, was another matter.

Standing in my living room I explained that perhaps one of the most direct paths to a better score is not to keep score. I told him that giving up results completely would free your mind and your potential—and by doing that, results would usually follow. I tried to explain it several different ways. Each time I was met with the same expression, which I'd never before seen on his face—as the wheels in his mind visibly turned, attempting to get his brain around the concept of not keeping score. As I spoke, his head shook involuntarily back and forth as if to say, "NO! NO! NO!!!! This goes against the laws of man!" Then he spoke.

"But, that's the whole point, isn't it? Shooting the lowest score. I mean what's the point otherwise?" he asked. Then added, gravely, "I'm going to need a bit of time with this one."

We could have taken the conversation into all kinds of philosophical directions. Because how much more of a metaphor for life and the conundrum of modern existence could you find than the question of what constitutes a life well lived, or what is the purpose of playing golf if it is not to keep score? How does one quantify their existence or measure its success? Is there really success in life? Is it a running tally of money, experiences, or holes-in-one? Or is it simply a "journey without goal," as Chogyam Rinpoche suggests? And if that's the case, what is the journey towards? Nothingness? Death? Can I break 80 on the way?

Big-ticket stuff—all of it. But, as Martin Heidegger was nowhere to be found and my dad looked as though I'd just dropped Carnie Wilson on his head, I decided to give him some space and changed the subject.

Because of the crappy weather I pretty much had Willow Hill to myself. On the par-4 first, I hit two decent 5-irons and was just short of the green. I chipped up with my 5-and two-putted for a bogey, but wrote nothing on my card. The second hole was a near exact repeat of the first. Two 5-s to about 20 feet from the apron, a chip, two putts, and another bogey.

As I dropped my putter back in my bag, I pulled the scorecard from my pocket and had an experience that I imagine mirrored that of an alcoholic who drives up to a bar and sits in the parking lot, shaky hands gripping the wheel, trying to determine whether or not he will fall off the wagon. I stood there with the pencil and card in my hands, no idea what to do, for a long time. Just like the alcoholic, I was experiencing a blur of contrasting images, those of the welcome comfort that the booze or scorecard represented set against the brighter path towards a better life and the powerful freedom offered by unshackling oneself from the scorecard. For a good ten minutes, I just couldn't put that damn pencil back in my pocket. Then, in a rare act of willpower, I did.

Standing on the tee at the 167-yard, par-3 third hole, I felt the wind at my back and decided to hit a very, very easy 5-. I walked to my ball and as Bolland had instructed, just went up, got comfortable, and hit without any thought. "Make your shot be your practice swing," he'd told me. I'm not even sure where the swing came from or where it started—it just happened. The ball flew straight at the pin, then past it, hitting the back of the green and bouncing off into the rough, maybe 185 yards from the tee. Here I felt the true freedom of not keeping score. I was thrilled. The shot felt great and was aesthetically beautiful. I wasn't caught up in thinking about how I was going to get up and down, nor did I expend energy wishing that I'd hit a 6- or 7-. Then I was interrupted.

"Can I join you?" asked a twenty-fiveish-year-old guy who looked as if he'd emerged full blown from the spring clearance sale at Golf Galaxy.

There is a moment in *Golf in the Kingdom*—during the long evening of dinner and drinks by the fire at the McNaughtons' house, where the mystical and mysterious lure of golf is debated and the game is eventually dubbed "The New Yoga of the Supermind"— where the lovely Agatha McNaughton explains that the primary allure of golf is that it is a way for men to show their love for each other and of being with each other and to essentially celebrate each other's beauty by saying "great shot," without getting all mushy, as the Beaver used to say. And I pretty much agree with her wholeheartedly, up to a point. My friends, my dad, and the occasional guy I pair up with can often prove the truth of her statement. But I've also found that the only way to make changes in my game is within the solitude of playing by myself, where I can get my bearings. I have also realized that when alone, I can make a round of golf something of a meditation. When I am alone I can see the first glimpses of how it can be a positive act of self-realization, rather than four hours of running headlong into my demonic ego. That said, I asked him to join me.

The young man introduced himself as the assistant pro at Willow Hill and then—in a moment when I swear Shivas Irons, Buddha, and Champagne Tony Lema were laughing at me from above—explained that he was also a divinity student at a local seminary.

On this day, however, God was not on his side and I outplayed him as we finished nine and then played the course a second time.

The most memorable moment, however, came on the sixth or seventh hole, when he looked at me and—with all the earnestness of a divinity student—said, "I'm sure you hear this all the time, but you've got a beautiful swing."

In fact, I'd never heard that before. I may well have blushed.

o o o o

Perhaps it is the dearth of MacHorwitzes in the Edinburgh phone book or the fact that the diminutive Corey Pavin is the greatest Jewish golfer in PGA history that is responsible for the fact that in the Judeo-Christian tradition, the Judeo end of the bargain really has made no contribution to the literature of golf, God, and how the two come together. Yes, there is *When Bad Things Happen to Good People*, but, frankly, I'm not terribly interested in bad things happening to just about anyone, aside from Cubs fans, who deserve every bit of suffering they experience in their miserable, pathetic lives.

The Christians, however, have more than made up for the lack of output among the golfing Jewry. I love to say and write that word—Jewry. I'll do it again. Jewry.

The titles from the "Jesus is my homeboy" contingent run the gamut from *God Plays Golf* to *And God Created Golf*. But, from a perspective of pure reason, did God not also create the sun, the wind, the trees, and Dave Coulier? If so, he has a bit of explaining to do. I think he made a few mistakes.

Some of these books take Bible passages and reinterpret them to suit your game; others, like *In His Grip*, explain that God wants to be a coach who simultaneously helps you win at both golf and life. Some have a sense of humor.[1] Others do not. Nearly all, however, have a foreword, preface, or introduction written by the PGA Tour's foremost born-again Christian, Tom Lehman, who must be the kindest, most thoughtful man in the world. I, however, vastly prefer the books where a prominent theologian—like Pat Boone—weighs in on God and golf.

My favorite amongst these is Billy Graham's surprisingly funny and astute intro for *In His Grip*, where he discusses those who suggest that the apostle Paul was referring to golf when he wrote, "I have fought a good fight. I have finished the course." To which Billy replies, "I think that suggestion is definitely up for theological debate!"

The humor is all in the exclamation points.

I think the primary reason that the only books about golf and spirituality written by Jews are written by converts to

---

1 If you are compelled to delve into this area, I highly recommend Father Mike Linder's *Play It as It Lies*, whose intro asks the question that has stuck in the back of my mind during this entire journey, simply—because of his transcendent golfing prowess, was Jack Nicklaus the most enlightened, spiritually aware man of the twentieth century?

Buddhism like Doc Parent is the nature of the religion itself. Judaism is many things, but to me it is mostly a blueprint for living a good and moral. life. And in this way I think it's fantastic. But, there are two things that I never found during the horrific stretch of my life during which my parents conducted some kind of bizarre religious experiment by sending me, their first born, to a Conservative temple for Hebrew and Sunday school.

Conservative Judaism sits in that netherworld between Reform and Orthodox. When I was very young I remember a relative describing the difference between the three as being: lazy (Reform), crazy (Orthodox), and hazy (Conservative). In my experience, however, there was nothing hazy about my religious education, which included Tuesday and Thursday afterschool Hebrew instruction (a time when I'd have far preferred to be playing strikeout with my friends) from scary Israeli women who appeared to have killed several people that morning and had yet to solidify their plans for the afternoon. The only relief came in the way of my friend Allen Klein's ability to fart on command during class. It was cold comfort.

And comfort is something I really wanted from religion. But instead of getting to play catch and sing with the ever mellow Der Bingle in a Jewish version of "Going My Way," I was left with a rich tradition of neuroses that owed more to Larry David than Father O'Malley. In retrospect, I can see this was my problem—not Judaism's.

Ultimately, I just never got the hang of Judaism. It was too amorphous, the services were too long, and my parents—particularly my mother—weren't religious enough to justify a

Conservative upbringing. By the time I was done, my brother was enrolled at a temple that was so Reform the services were practically in Latin.

I think my paternal grandmother was truly my most kindred spiritual forbear, with a philosophy best summed up by her comment upon being asked if she enjoyed my marathon-length Bar Mitzvah: "Enjoy it!!! I thought I was going to die!!!"

With that preamble, these days I probably identify myself with Jewish culture more than I ever have. But, I did not suspect that eighteen holes with a rabbi would ever bring me back into the fold spiritually. Mostly, I felt it was important to be reminded of from whence I came and to see if I could better understand where I was headed.

o o o o

I was smacking 5-irons off the practice tee at Presidio Golf Course in San Francisco on a clear, cool morning. Totally fluid. Completely effortless. And then my phone rang.

"Joshua, it's Rabbi Strulowitz. I'm running late."

It rang again shortly thereafter.

"Joshua, it's Rabbi Strulowitz. Traffic is bad, but I think I'll make it on time."

And a third time.

"Joshua, I'm here; could you pick me up on the parking lot?"

There are two kinds of people in the world who call me Joshua. One is my father. The other is pretty much any rabbi that I encounter.

Having a fellow Joshua call me Joshua is something I found rather endearing, made all the more so by the fact that Rabbi Joshua Strulowitz is twelve years my junior.

Now, I had already been through the "I'm a grown-up" ringer, made apparent not so much by doing things like getting married, having kids, buying a house, and purchasing life insurance as experiencing the lawyer who did my closing being younger than me; or remembering the two attractive, young female interns, who looked as though they were high school seniors, being brought in to watch me receive a full physical in a very cold room; or the mom of one of my son's friends, who told me that my next door neighbor's (a fortyish mom of four) youngest sister had been her high school soccer coach. I'd gone from thinking college basketball players seemed to be my age to looking at NBA veterans who now appeared to be quite a bit younger than me. But, I guess I was just never expecting a rabbi who hadn't yet walked when I first listened to *Cheap Trick Live* at Budokan.

The rabbi was lacing up his shoes and gathering up his golf gear from the trunk when I arrived to pick him up. He wore glasses, a beard, and a Florida Marlins hat. As the bishop in *Caddyshack* laments to Judge Smales, he is "just a man" like the rest of us.

At the first tee, we were paired up with an investment adviser playing nine holes of hooky and a Presidio regular named Tony, who was a Chinese retiree somewhere in his sixties. When he teed off, I could immediately identify the kind of golfer Tony was. His swing had the mechanics of someone really flexible trying to crack a whip after having taken too many Quaaludes. He would always be twenty yards behind everyone off the tee, but he would always hit it straight, land in the fairway, and be putting for par on every hole.

The rabbi and I were not quite as mature. Both of us hit slashing drives that went about 220 and wide right toward the driving range. As it was the first hole, we both took an Eisenberg and hit decent drives that landed in the short fringe on the opposite sides of the fairway. Both of us got on in 4 and double-bogeyed.

Though we barely knew each other, the rabbi and I fell quickly into easy conversation about golf, our wives, children, and careers. I asked him if his parents had wanted him to be a rabbi, only to find that—like mine—they envisioned him as a lawyer, doctor, or businessperson.

"Anything but a rabbi," he said.

On the par-4 second, I asked if he had known he wanted to be a rabbi from a young age, and whether he'd felt the presence of God as a child.

"All kids are spiritual," he told me. "We get cynical as we get older."

For me, that process began in second grade, when I was just as likely to fervently believe that Patty Duke had an identical cousin as I was to accept the existence of God in my life.

Early on, I had developed my own brand of agnosticism—which basically was a belief in God motivated by my fear of not believing in God. I also had created a complex philosophy of God's will that I hoped would free me from Hebrew and Sunday School, namely that God was a good guy, not given to hypocrisy, time wasting, or the kind of "worship me" quality one associates with lesser beings, like Kobe Bryant. Instead, the last thing he wanted was for anyone to go—against their will—to some random building to prove to Him how much we loved Him and believed in Him. I thought the exact opposite was true. His vision was for us to follow the big commandments that He gave to Moses, and the rest was in our hands. He believed in me, no matter what, so long as it could get me out of Hebrew school.

Never worked.

Though I never outright explained that philosophy to him, the rabbi seemed like a guy who could handle it, pointing out that there is a difference between "religious" and "observant."

By the third hole, the rabbi had told me that he was having trouble with both his 6-iron and his putting, the latter of which he said that he had "no confidence in at all in." Strong words, which made it all the more heartening on the fifth, when he drained an 18-footer and then did the bent-legged, fist-pumping Tiger "YES!!!" move.

We bogeyed, occasionally doubled, and parred our way around the front nine and came into the turn at 47 (me) and 50 (the rabbi). The investment guy said his goodbyes and Tony pressed on with Rabbi Strulowitz and me. Both were excellent company.

I became even more thankful for the rabbi's presence on the back, when for the first six holes our woe was biblical if nothing else. Job would have cried if he triple bogeyed as many holes as we did.

It was hard to discern what happened. I had been swinging fairly well all day, but just not getting results. And some swings were resulting in horrifically bad shots. I stood there on several occasions totally dumbfounded at how my new swing—so recently declared "beautiful" by a golf pro/divinity student—

could be rendering such frighteningly awful grounders, popups, and shanks. The rabbi was right there with me.

At one point, I gave serious consideration to looking up into the sky and—like Murphy giving God the finger on the front nine at Burningbush—screaming, "HAVE THE JEWS NOT SUFFERED ENOUGH?!!"

In the midst of this calamitous streak, we began talking about the difference between Judaism and other religions, in which you are often asked to do things with no better explanation than "because."

"The Jews, we'll give you thirty different answers to the same question, but never 'because,'" he told me, understanding that this was both humorous and one of the wonderful qualities of Judaism. To have it any other way would be counter to the entire history of our people.

Now, I happen to be a guy who loves "because." Though I'm not a joiner, I always perceived that religion would be a lot easier if there were less thinking to do. I did not know that I would find that via Buddhism and meditation—but from early on I wanted to just know that things were the way they were because that's the way it was.

A perfect illustration of how Judaism takes the opposite approach came a few years ago during the High Holidays when my brother and I got into an argument about whether Jews believed in heaven. He said yes; I said no. That's what I had always been taught. He said that he'd learned there was a heaven—and that things might have changed in the three years that divided us. As both of us were fallen Jews, we put in a call to my dad, who was driving home from temple.

Me: "Dad, there's no heaven; at least Jews don't believe in one, right?"

My dad: "Maybe there's a heaven."

Me: "What!!! Maybe there's a heaven? Didn't you always tell me that there was no heaven?"

My dad: "I might have."

Me: "Then how can there suddenly be heaven?"

My dad: "What can I say, now, maybe there's a heaven."

Me: "But, you told me there was no heaven; how is there a heaven now?"

My dad: "Listen, maybe there's a heaven. That's all I can tell you. Things change sometimes. Maybe. Then again, maybe not."

Judaism is many things, but I can safely say it is hardly the opiate of the masses, unless those masses are inclined to step into a theological version of "Who's on First?"

o o o o

When we reached the sixteenth tee, the rabbi had to leave and attend to a synagogue event that evening. Both of us had tripled at least three of the six holes on the back. And neither of us had parred even one.

He was a good guy and we'd talked much more about life in general than about "life" itself. I could tell he was waiting for me to ask the big questions, for which he'd have thirty or more answers. But I couldn't do it. I could see that we were alike, only that he was much younger and considerably more religious. And God, it would seem, wasn't terribly concerned with either of our games.

That said, there was one other profound difference between us two Joshuas—I had no sense that it had ever occurred to him that his performance on the course was in any way reflective of his value as a human being. I was just now coming to that realization about myself.

Somehow, amidst the horrors of those first six holes on the back nine, I had managed to neither implode nor think I was a bad golfer and—by extension—a worthless human being because of my deficiencies on the course. Instead, I'd managed to stay in the mindset of trying to make good swings and accepting that sometimes nothing works.

We shook hands and I strapped my bag onto Tony's cart. Then something remarkable happened.

Like the woman at Genpo Roshi's seminar at Kripalu, I had—for the moment—given up searching. For real. It was just Tony and I standing there on the tee at the sixteenth, an uphill par-4. After Tony hit his usual 210-yard dead center drive, I teed one up and hit my longest drive of the day, just over a fairway trap and into the rough on the right. It was the best result I'd had from any swing since we'd made the turn. I suddenly felt calm. I wasn't trying to do anything. I was just out hitting golf balls on a nice day.

My second shot was from about 160 and needed to sail over two traps guarding a narrow entryway to the green. I grabbed my 6-iron, got comfortable, and had my best swing of the day. I didn't care where it landed or what happened. It just felt good. I'd been trying to make that my intention all day, but suddenly it was easy.

Because it was a blind shot over the traps, I had no idea where my ball was, but only that it had cleared the traps and I assumed the result would be a good one, which it was. The ball was 3 feet past the hole and a bit to the right. My birdie putt touched the left edge and stayed there. I tapped in for par. I had played the hole shot for shot—remaining in the present. I was not angry or disappointed at missing my birdie putt. Instead, if I have learned nothing else, it is to be thankful for tap-in pars—or any pars for that matter.

On seventeen, another par-4, I drove it straight down the middle for the first time that day. Then Tony spoke.

"You're a good golfer," he said. "You're just starting out the season, right?"

Okay, how can I not love a man who excuses my bad play for me?

When I hit an easy, smooth mid-iron to about 10 feet from the hole, he smiled.

"Do you know what I like about the way you play golf?" he asked. "You swing the club. You don't hit the ball. You have a beautiful swing and you just swing. Even when you are hitting it badly. That's what the pros do."

This was the second time in two rounds that my swing had been recognized for its newfound beauty. It took all of my courage to avoid asking him to come back to Chicago with me and become my Bagger Vance.

Again my first putt was close, and I tapped in for another par.

Standing on the tee at eighteen, a 516-yard par-5, my mind was clear. Tony and I shot the shit as we took a few warm-up swings. My drive was long, but imperfect, off to the right and into the rough that ran inside of a long stand of ancient trees. The 3-iron I hit from there was as lovely a shot as I've ever hit.

I used very little energy, held the club as loosely as possible, and launched one 210 yards and back into the center of the fairway.

From 55 yards, I pulled out my 60-degree wedge and then kind of blacked out—like Tiger not remembering that he even took the club from the bag. Before I knew it, I had plopped a high shot over a greenside trap and landed it on the front of the green, 4 feet uphill and left of the pin.

Now this is the point where I am supposed to be anticipating the big finish. It's the moment when I view this putt as redemption—the birdie that proves to me that I can still play this game and that I'm truly a single-digit handicap trapped inside of this bogey-golfing body and mind. Or the alternative, where I start pre-planning for my failure. It is where I say to myself, "Even if you miss the birdie, you make par. And even if you miss par, you bogey and one over for the last three holes is just fine."

But, I really didn't care. It was one of the first moments on a golf course that I can recall my ego being completely out of the way. I was simply spending a nice afternoon on the course with my new friend Tony, whose personality is like butter melting on a waffle and I was all the more thankful for it.

As Tony putted out, I rooted for him to make par. Then I stepped to my ball. The putt was tricky, downhill on fast greens with a turn to the right. I swung my putter back and forth in my hands, which barely held the club. Only one thought was in my mind—comfort. Somewhere behind that, however, I had no doubt that I would sink this putt. And I did.

Tony and I rode to the parking lot together. Lest you think he is some incarnation of Buddha sent to put me on the right path, I must tell you he was raised Catholic and is a graduate of Marquette, with a Franciscan monk in the family. Nor is he a

Confucian riddle master. Instead, he's just a nice guy whose family came here from China when he was a young boy, and who possesses an easy manner, quirky swing, and the ability to laugh at anything.

As he got in his car and pulled away, I noticed that I was still there—mentally. I was not thinking back on my round nor grasping at the future. I was just there. And in that moment I realized that culturally I will always be Jewish, but that those three holes with Tony were a clear sign to me—I was right in looking Eastward for both my spiritual home and my golf game.

Somehow amidst the wreckage and disappointment of some really bad golf, I was able to experience a three-hole manifestation of my best self. I was egoless, calm, present, and relaxed. I was detached from results, sank my putts, and effortlessly hit mid-irons to 10 feet. That, I hope and believe, is the real me.

Now, the question is, how do I find and remain that guy? I was prepared to play the best golf of my life. Perhaps, however, I should have read a bit further in *Golfing with God*, where Herman Fins-Winston says the following:

"I felt somehow unprepared to look God in the face that day. Unworthy. Later, I would learn something about that kind of shame. It is that exact feeling, exactly that sense of unworthiness, that forms the fertile ground from which most spiritual troubles sprout. Trite as it may sound, the fact is that the Being that created us loves us, approves of us, expects the best from us. . . . So often in the whirl of earth, amidst the complexities of family life and our professional ambitions, we lose sight of that existential approval. We turn away from that love. And after that, well, . . . no place to go but down."

CHAPTER
10

Zen, Ox Herding, and How I Played the Best Golf of My Life Without Being Murdered by My Wife

Using intellectual understanding to find your true nature is like expecting a hungry man to satisfy his gnawing hunger with a picture of a banana. Zen teaching is not like this. Zen teaching says, "Open your mouth. Here's a banana. Now eat!"

—ZEN MASTER SEUNG SAHN

SUMMER 2008. CHICAGO, ILLINOIS / PRINCETON, NEW JERSEY

When I returned from San Francisco, if my scores were any indication, I was not fully prepared to accept that God loved me, or even that I loved myself, much less my putter. My trajectory was not downwards. Instead, it was more like sideways, or better yet, a zigzag. In fact, if my game reflected my inner state, one would have to conclude that I had become bipolar. I was the golfing equivalent of Faye Dunaway at the end of *Chinatown*: "my sister, my daughter, my sister, my daughter." It was not my favorite place to be.

I would shoot 41 on the front and 49 on the back. I would shoot 50 on the front and 42 on the back. My game had entered a bizarre phase, where I was skulling short irons on the par–3s where I tended to play my best, at the same time that I was blasting 225-yard 3-woods off the deck and getting close to the green in 2 on par–5s. Up was down. Hot was cold.

On at least three occasions I ate up the front nine at Glencoe, where I was usually thrilled to shoot 44, only to implode on the first six holes of the back, a stretch where I could always depend on playing my best golf.

Somehow, as this was transpiring, I remembered to tell myself that it was part of the journey, while ignoring the bad holes and reasoning that the good holes were the real me. I also began to figure something out.

The bad holes, the bad nines, the bad everything happened when I was trying to do too much. They occurred when I had a plan. My primary sin had transferred from sloth to pride. Thus, if I arrived at the course with a desire to play well, the front would be a disaster. If I played great on the front and came into the back thinking that I might, just might, be able to get down near 80, I would fall apart. I'd swing too hard, or too soft, I'd be in my head instead of my body. I'd be focused on results, rather than process. This, I realized, was what I had to master.

Perhaps the most vivid reflection of this arose one sweltering day with my father at Northmoor Country Club. As I drove to the Donald Ross–designed layout, where millions had been invested to make it even more brutal and challenging than the Scottish master had ever imagined, I was feeling what I assumed was Doc Parent's "unconditional confidence." I was going to kick some ass in the name of Buddha and finally show my dad and two of his friends just how remarkable a golfing Zen master I'd become.

Standing on the first tee, I was intent on floating above the fairways, descending only to demonstrate my Snead-like swing and a detachment from results that would lead to my transcendence on the scorecard.

I doubled the first. "Fuck it," I said to myself. I did that all the time. I was not concerned. I bogeyed the second, a long, narrow par-5. Not bad, I thought. I was within myself. I was letting things come to me. And then I entered golfing hell

On three, I hit a nice drive that split the middle, but followed it with a low liner hybrid shot that left me 75 yards short in the left rough with a tricky wedge shot to an elevated and absurdly protected green. My intense focus on hitting a Mickelsonesque masterpiece with my 60-degree wedge led to three consecutive worm burners. I tripled.

At the par-3 fourth, I hit my 4-hybrid to the back of the green and was lucky to get down in four putts from 20 feet. From there it got worse. I was incapable of hitting two good shots in a row. The holes suddenly felt as if they were 600 yards long. I could see nothing but the hazards or the confusing contours of each green. I switched putters. I continually asked for whatever club I absolutely shouldn't be using. I went for it every time, no matter where I was. My caddy, a teenaged Mexican kid whose job was to pretend that guys like me were worthy of having their bags carried, shook his head nonstop, even when he knew I was watching.

On the ninth, I needed a par to make 50. I doubled.

Sweating, I stood on the tenth tee chugging a Gatorade while my dad and his friends hit the washroom. This gave me a moment to think. I tried to slow my mind and get my bearings. I told myself that if I could just calm down I would be able to loosen my grip, clear my head, and do something that would bring back the guy who was 1-under on the last three at Presidio.

When I teed up my ball on the long par-5, I had every intention of doing all of those things. I promptly hit it 250 yards straight down the middle—of the next fairway.

Breathing deeply, I engaged the same mindset on my second shot, a 3-wood that went 190 and landed in a clump of trees separating the fairways.

I looked at my ball and realized that I couldn't go low and didn't want to punch backwards to get on the fairway. My only option, I decided, was totally insane—hitting a wedge that would rise immediately and miss every one of hundreds of twigs, leaves, and branches between my ball and the green.

Taking a breath, I thought of a recently deceased friend of my father's—an avid and terrible golfer, who used to approach such a shot and say of the trees that they are "90 percent air."

Standing over my ball, I opened my hands up completely, letting my club almost float there. I flexed my fingers and put them back loosely around the grip. I sat back a bit into my ass, finding balance and, without another thought, had my first good swing of the day. The ball soared straight up, missing every bit of wood and vegetation in its way before lightly clipping two leaves as it headed towards the sky, causing it to die perfectly on the back of the green, 14 feet behind the hole. From there I two-putted for par.

As we walked to the eleventh, something inside of me changed. Based on having hit two shots wildly off course, then having been rescued by a low-percentage shot better suited to Seve in his prime—and coming out with a par—I made a mental shift. I began to truly understand the folly and illusion of making plans and believing in control. I tossed myself to the fates, and immediately the thought of chasing a score on the back—one that would make up for the horror of the front—was gone. In its place was something unfamiliar. It was a sense of adventure. I really didn't care what I shot. And not in that reckless, fuck-it-all kind of way, but in a different, healthy, fuck-it-all kind of way. I realized that I couldn't go back and do anything about that 52 any more than Pedro could have avoided tossing Don Zimmer on his big stupid metal-plated head. Stuff happens and it's over. That is the nature of life. What was done was done. Life didn't let you do it over, but what it did let you do was move forward and meet the next challenge. And—more importantly—it allowed you to (as much as it pains me to type these words) be here now.

I would, I decided, integrate my *Tao* (the path) and *Te* (character) to bring about a union that sounds amazingly simple, but becomes more and more difficult with each passing year. I would become one with nature and essentially be okay with both the good and the bad that I faced—viewing them as a whole, unified entity, rather than separate forces of positive and negative. To achieve it, however, I would need to be fully present, which is very simple—and undeniably impossible.

But, on this journey, I had learned a trick. To become present and acceptant of all that occurs, you have to do one simple thing—you must *do*, rather than *try*.

So, what is doing, as opposed to trying? Well, that's a problem. But, here's my best shot. When you are doing, you are not thinking nor are you focused on a goal. Instead, you are acting in a manner that derives pleasure from the action, rather than its consequence. Yes, it's a lot like being in the zone, but it's also more than that. It's being comfortable with whatever result might occur. It is detachment from the vagaries of positive and negative.

And if you're a visual learner, rent the movie *High Society*, a musical retelling of *The Philadelphia Story* with Grace Kelly in the Katharine Hepburn role, Frank Sinatra taking over for Jimmy Stewart, and Bing Crosby as the laid-back playboy jazz musician C. K. Dexter Haven, portrayed by Cary Grant in the original.

Pay particular attention to a party scene where Frank and Bing sing a duet entitled "Well, Did You Evah!" Frank, God love him, is an entertainment machine. He is dancing his ass off, singing intensely, and playing drunk with a subtlety just this side of Foster Brooks—all with complete consciousness that he is in a movie and that he is going to give you every dime's worth. He is like Al Pacino in a musical version of *Devil's Advocate*.

Then there is Bing. He barely moves. He sits down while Frank sings. He smokes a cigarette and—for no good reason— taps a cork into a bottle with his elbow. He does a few takes, singing like a man who hasn't a care in the world yet wants to get the girl, but will be all right if someone sets him on fire. There is not a trace of self-consciousness or effort. And he blows Frank off the screen, because he is not *trying* to be anything but Bing Crosby playing C. K. Dexter Haven. He's just *doing*.

In golf, Phil is *trying* when he goes to the site of the next major a month ahead of time and plots out every bump and contour, planning where he'll hit every shot. That worked for Hogan, but he was an anal little bastard who was born to do things like walk the course backwards. It came naturally to him. That was Hogan *doing*. It was an expression of his self-knowledge. For a big, talented, imperfect and genial master of the daring escape like Phil—it's just a lot of trying.

Ultimately, trying is all about making a greater effort, particularly one that seems to be pushing your energy outward. Doing is drawing just a tiny bit inward, where the true power really resides. It's trying less and getting more. It's what makes your body think and your mind act.

This is where I was on the back.

In all fairness, I must also note that I told my caddy that under no circumstances was he to give me that 60-degree wedge—no matter how much I begged, pleaded, or threatened to tie him up and make him watch *Beaches*. And while the adventure began with a 7-iron into the drink on the par-3 eleventh, I dropped my second attempt on the green and curled in an 8-footer. From there each shot was what it was. I rarely thought about what was going to happen. I was in the moment and—more importantly—it wasn't fleeting. It wasn't about being in the zone. It wasn't coming and going. There was no work involved. I was simply there and doing.

On the eighteenth, a long par-4, I drilled my tee shot over the left edge of the large trap on the right and hit a downhill slope leaving me about 180 yards from the green. I got to my ball and looked at the green, which I'd hit in regulation in maybe four or five of the more than sixty times I'd played the hole. I pulled out my 4-hybrid and aimed a bit left. The ball flew straight until about 20 yards before the green, where it began arcing gently back to the right and landed 8 feet from the hole. From there I narrowly missed a birdie putt that would have brought me in at under 40 for the first time in my life. But, on this day I would not curse fate. Instead, I smiled at the discrepancy between 52 and 40.

A week later, I was off to see the abbot.

o o o o

Yes, I did begin this book intent on playing with the Sakyong Mipham Rinpoche, the leader of Shambhala. The Sakyong, however, didn't share this desire. I never spoke to him directly, working instead through his minions. There was his scheduler, his publicity person, and ultimately one of his golf buddies, whom I courted with an embarrassing level of ardor.

All of these minions were very nice. They all kept saying that if the Sakyong had time, something might be arranged. But there were complications. The Sakyong got married. His wife became pregnant. He had all kinds of Sakyong-oriented stuff to do. It just wasn't going to happen.

At first, I was in some bizarre state of disbelief. The kind one feels when a pretty good relationship ends and you don't fully grasp that it is indeed over. I kept after the golf buddy. Like any self-respecting ex, he stopped answering my calls and emails. A good reporter, I told myself, doesn't give up on a source. A man on a quest, I also remembered, doesn't quit simply because another party has yet to understand the importance of what he seeks. Like a man spurned, I told myself these lies. But one day, when I had sent the last of twenty or so unanswered emails, I came to the realization that my behavior bordered somewhat on stalking and that stalking a Buddhist holy man was bad form, while doing so through one of his golf partners was just plain sad.

Thus, I headed to Google, seeking a substitute cleric who would join me for some self-exploration on the fairways of life. And this is where I found the writings of Abbot John on the Web site Zatma.org. The first words of his that I read were these:

"I have always been uncomfortable with the literary habit of coupling Zen Buddhism with every sport known to man. There's a Zen of tennis and a Zen of running, a Zen of baseball, and so on, ad infinitum. We never find the Judaism of skiing, the Catholicism of volleyball, the Sufism of curling. Why Zen, I have repeatedly asked myself. Are we sports' psychologists?

"And then, as I've previously admitted, I took up golf."

I'd found my abbot.

I emailed John. He responded in the witty, sardonic, and cantankerous voice of his articles that took on not only golf, but also dealt with common suburban matters, like his murderous impulses towards a haughty interior decorator.

He was a member, I found out, of the order of Hsu Yun, an online, but completely legitimate, Zen Buddhist ministry. A bit of research led me to find that Hsu Yun was a Ch'an meditation master who supposedly lived for 120 years—finally shedding this mortal coil in 1959.

John was open to playing golf, but was understandably circumspect. He warned me that he was a bit more "churlish" than your average Zen abbot, which I considered further reason for getting together. I was excited to find someone who was both a Zen master and a normal person who could admit that other people still occasionally bugged the crap out of him. He was a guy who seemed to own his own shit.

A plan was hatched: I would visit him in New Jersey in late July, when we would play two days of golf—the first would be a charity outing supporting an organization that sent care packages to members of the 82nd Airborne (of which one of his sons is a member), followed by a daylong "play all you can" extravaganza at his usual course. Thus, on a blazing hot day I boarded a plane for Philly, then drove to Princeton, New Jersey, to meet the abbot.

o o o o

Our first encounter was in the Yankee Doodle Bar and Grille in the basement of Princeton's Nassau Inn. There, under photos of esteemed Princeton alumni like Dean Cain, Brooke Shields, and Donald Rumsfeld, the abbot and I ate waffles and chewed the metaphysical fat.

I found the abbot at a small lacquered-wood table, drinking coffee, chomping on Nicorette, and looking for all the world like a conventional suburban businessman who liked to play golf. His nearly bald head was deeply tanned and there was a Buddha belly beneath his blue polo. But what was most striking about Abbot John was his voice.

I had expected something low and rumbling. Perhaps the voice of a veteran character actor who played amusing film heavies. I was not prepared for a soft, twangy Southern concoction born of rural Indiana and Texas. And as I listened to this unexpected voice I learned how Abbot John became Abbot John.

John's interest in spirituality and becoming a cleric goes back to the Vietnam War, which he spent in a Franciscan seminary. But when he emerged, John took a decidedly non-Franciscan path, marrying a Jewish woman (and a lovely one at that) from Baltimore, having twin sons, and leading an altogether secular, conventional lifestyle. A determined, self-made man, albeit a somewhat iconoclastic Bob Dylan–quoting one, he built a successful manufacturing business and pretty much attained the American dream.

And it was that American dream that led John on the path to abbothood. Because it was that American dream that led John to what he calls a "dark night of the soul." This event took place in John's kitchen one day in the mid-1990s, as he contemplated the fact that he had everything. And while John appreciated that he had everything, and was glad that he had everything, he wondered whether there was something more than a good business, a nice house, a loving family, and a new car every two years. I imagine most upper-middle-class and white-collar folks have this moment at some point, and that the majority wait until that moment passes. But, to John's credit, he did not. Instead, he issued a challenge to God, asking for the Big Man to step up and show some proof of His existence.

That proof, John told me, came not in the form of a burning bush, nor a set of stone tablets. It came not in a vision, nor from a winged messenger. Instead, just like Hal Holbrook's oracle-like stockbroker appeared in Wall Street to explain that when man looks into the abyss he sees himself, an investment adviser called John that very day and said he was "in the neighborhood," as investment advisers so frequently find themselves, and asked if he could drop by.

When the investment adviser popped in he asked how John was doing. It is a question that people rarely answer with anything approaching honesty. But John is a man who is nothing if not completely honest about how he perceives the world. So, he told him about his existential quandary. Then, instead of explaining how small-caps or the new index fund from Morgan Stanley was just the answer to his spiritual ennui, the stockbroker went to his car and returned with several books about Buddhism that had been given to him by his previous client. Talk about your mountain coming to Mohammed.

As I imagine he does with anything that captures his imagination and interest, John threw himself into Buddhism, which led to meditation, which led to some lifestyle shifts, and ultimately to the point where he was asked to become an abbot. Like Groucho, John didn't want to be part of any club that would have him as a member, but ultimately gave in. And thus was born Abbot John.

o o o o

When we finish breakfast, John looks at his watch and says that there is some extra time before we need to head to the course. He suggests we take a walk around Princeton's Cotswold Gothic campus. Before long we pass a church where John would go meditate back in the day. Going inside he points out where his wife would sit, mortified, as he chanted loudly in the cavernous sanctuary, not caring who heard him or what anyone thought. I think somehow the abbot was always inside of John and simply needed to be released.

At some point after we leave the church, John casually mentions having achieved satori. I ask him what it's like. In a slow drawl, with a half-smile, he tells me that your ego moves out of the way and the mind becomes like a piece of clear glass instead of a windswept ocean. It's a mixed metaphor, but I get it.

Then we stop and he says, "It's indescribable and people ask you to describe it. But that would make it not so indescribable, right?"

o o o o

Cherry Valley Golf club is located in one of those *Truman Show*–style subdivisions with a golf twist, where all of the streets have names like Palmer Lane, Shoal Creek Drive, and Fairway Avenue. The course itself is pristine and the front nine is just an ungodly bitch—with gigantic greens that are two- and three-tiered monstrosities with dips, turns, and everything but quicksand and deadly pythons.

Upon arriving, I meet John's wife, who is running the event; we then go have a second breakfast in the clubhouse. At my table is a big, muscle-bound guy who sells patriotic logo golf shirts. When I am asked what I do, he gives me a curious look that says, "You seem like too decent a guy to be part of the liberal mainstream media." A few minutes later, he gives me a death-grip handshake and we part ways. He, undoubtedly, to hit 300-yard drives. I, to purchase a cigar as my way of showing that I support the troops as much as the next guy.

Finding John outside, I meet the two other members of our foursome, Eric and Marc. The former is a big, affable, hard-swinging guy who works for John, and the latter, one of Eric's old friends. Both are intelligent, in their mid-to-late forties, and great company. We make a relaxed, convivial foursome that demonstrates early on that it has no chance of winning the "captain's scramble" format (everyone hits from the group's best drive) tournament.

That, however, does not stop John from giving everyone a ton of shit. Missed putts and bad shots are universally condemned in arch screw-you-buddy fashion—and when he and I both get hot on the back nine, simultaneously dropping birdie putts on the same hole, Marc's and Eric's lesser efforts do not go without comment.

John has a nice swing for a guy who took up the game in his fifties and he seems to be one of those golfers who has made up for any of his deficiencies with a good mental game and the admirable, uncanny ability to score no matter what.

Our discussion of spiritual matters is minimal. At one point, however, John explains that in a traditional Zen monastery the two most important people are the abbot and the cook, which makes for all kinds of food prep parables that often do a good job of explaining how even the most mundane tasks are a venue for spiritual practice. The doing of dishes, chopping of wood, slaughtering of an ox, all done in the most conscious, present way humanly possible.

The other instance is when our balls are both down in a fairly deep valley with a steep drop from the fairway—the kind you would shoot your cart down when you were seventeen but in your forties you imagine how long it might put you in traction.

These thoughts do not trouble the abbot, who guns the cart straight downwards and says to me with a wry smile, "Well, you wanted to meet God, right?"

o o o o

We finish the round soaked in sweat, coming in as follows: me 89; Marc 80; Eric 86; John 81.

As we grab a beer, Marc and Eric ask me a question whose answer I assumed they already knew: "Just how do you know John anyway?"

When I tell them I'm a writer doing a book about golf and spirituality, writing a chapter about playing with John, they smile and laugh, as if it's the most normal thing in the world that someone is there to write about John.

What is remarkable about John is how his being an abbot and pursuing a very nontraditional means of spirituality, particularly in suburban New Jersey, is not something freaky to two very normal guys who know him. In fact, you can hear the genuine reverence and affection in Eric's voice when he talks about John. Underneath his caustic humor and monk-meets–H. L. Mencken persona, John is a powerful character, someone whose very behavior and embrace of something out of the mainstream can legitimize it and make others respect it without his ever having to say a word.

o o o o

The following morning we run over to John's home course, Mattawang. Straightforward but challenging, its fairways and greens are a bit shaggy, a stark contrast to the insanely manicured turf at Cherry Valley. The aesthetic extends to the clubhouse, where an employee kids me that their motto is "Your comfort is not our concern."

One thing seems eminently clear—John is far happier at Mattawang.

On the first tee he bangs one down the right side of the fairway. I stand up and rip mine down the middle. The day before I had been victim to my bad habit of slicing, pushing, and fading every drive. But, today I am in sync, my pace has slowed, and my drives are no longer impacted by my anxious desire to get to the ball as quickly as possible. I gain about 15 extra yards without the big arc and the need to aim for the left rough in order to hit a ball in the fairway.

"Old Josh has his driver out today," John drawls as my ball sails a bit past his.

I bogey, he pars.

On two, I hit a great 8-iron approach and par while he triples. We both par the long par-3 third. On four, I slam another long, straight drive. My second shot winds up off to the left of and below the elevated green, necessitating a delicate pitch onto a fairly small surface. The day before I'd told John that I much preferred this type of shot to a 40-foot putt I was standing over. He reminds me of this and says, "Well, I guess you just got your wish."

On the next hole, as he stands over a very, very long putt, John goes back to the same subject and before stroking his ball says that the shot "kind of gives you a queasiness in your testicles."

We are both playing fairly well and it's become a friendly, relaxed, but mildly competitive match. On a long par-5, I hit a nice drive and then a 3-wood that leaves me close to the green in 2. The abbot wonders aloud whether he should put the Buddha voodoo curse on me.

As we finish up eighteen with John in the low 80s and me at 88, we decide to play as much more golf as we can before the impending rain—during which I hope John will set me on the path of the righteous and one step further towards enlightenment.

We cut from hole to hole, avoiding any wait and every foursome we encounter. It becomes a golfing vision quest of sorts. When we replay the fourth, I hit a long drive that leaves me about 100 feet from the green and follow with a stiff wedge to about 8 inches for a tap-in birdie. But, the golf has become secondary.

We discuss philosophy and how "heaven and hell are right here on earth." This, however, doesn't stop John from busting my balls whenever he can. At one point we take up cheating on the scorecard and how it is the height of self-delusion. As the conversation begins to get deeper, I begin a sentence with, "I'm not big on morality, but . . ."

He cuts me off. "But you're moral where it really matters, like in golf, right?"

The most meaningful discussion is about satori and how to get there. John tells me that there is very little that you must do in order to find your way out of "the swamp" as he calls it. The answer, he says, is not a mile deep, but really just a tenth of an inch below the surface. But it is removing that tiny bit of protective skin or artifice that we most resist.

John is also refreshingly certain on the subject of gurus who promise a direct path to nirvana.

"You don't ascend those mountains in caravans," he says.

By the time we hit the last hole we are giddy. We each slash two or three drives apiece until we manage to get into the fairway. John finds one of his earlier drives in the rough and smashes a big 3-wood towards the green on this 426-yard, uphill par-4.

His shot lands 15 yards short. I stand over my ball and do the same, hitting a beautiful 3-wood that falls feet from John's.

The gray sky opens up as we hole out and a soft rain begins to fall. As we head to the parking lot, the rain gets steadier and steadier. John and I shake hands after we change our shoes. Then, stepping into his Lexus, he returns to his enlightened existence and I to the airport.

o o o o

I must admit that after I returned home, I missed John. He was a kindred spirit, someone whose spiritual enlightenment hadn't prevented him from seeing the idiocy not only in others, but also within himself. During those next weeks we emailed each other frequently, sometimes to talk spirituality, other times to share golf experiences, and others for no reason whatsoever. And then it happened. I finally dipped my toe in the holy waters of golfing satori.

Picasso had his Blue Period. The Beatles had the *White Album*. And the Yankees had 1927. My golf game? Well, it had August and September of 2008.

It began when the Sensei called to say that she was traveling through town and asked if I wanted to play eighteen holes with her and two friends. The date, August 8, was my wife's forty-first birthday, but she had stuff going on that afternoon, so I was set.

The reunion was a warm one. We hugged and I realized just how much affection had developed between us, and in some of the other relationships I'd developed through this quest. I met her friends, a husband and wife, and we teed off on the first hole at Chevy Chase Golf Club in Wheeling, Illinois.

My drive on the par-4 first went almost directly left and hit a chain link fence. I took a mulligan (something I hadn't done in months) and put one under a tree in the rough on the right. About 140 yards out, I punched a 4-hybrid that hit the left side of the green and curled upwards towards the hole. I dropped my putt for a mulligan birdie that I shamefully accepted.

The next six holes were awful. Doubles. Triples. Maybe a quad somewhere. I was miserable and desperate. Only nervous, teetering-on-the-edge pars on eight and nine kept me under 50. I was at 48 heading into the turn. Then, without warning, my brain switched off completely. I can't explain why; maybe it was the cumulative effect of my journey, maybe it was divine providence, or perhaps I'd found my authentic swing, but whatever the case I became deeply relaxed. I was following my breath, but not through conscious effort. Somehow my mind and lungs were just synced.

I parred. I parred again and again and again until I bogeyed fourteen and fifteen. I hit the green in regulation on both holes and each time left my par putt resting on the lip. Then I parred sixteen and seventeen. My mind did its best to churn. I began looking at my scorecard. I wasn't just about to break 40, I realized. If I birdied the par-5 eighteenth, I was going to come in at 1-over for the back, and, truthfully, for the last eleven holes.

The Sensei had figured out that I was on a run about three holes before, but didn't realize the gravity of the situation until I turned to her on the eighteenth tee and said, "I think I'm about to break 40."

I then teed up my ball and hit one long and just off the fairway to the left. Regrettably, however, my path to the green was blocked by an extremely tall tree that became very wide just at the point where I needed to hit my ball. In retrospect, I don't recall if I decided to go over the tree or around it. I do know that in one of those strange accidents my 3-hybrid started way left and then began to simultaneously climb and turn right—heading directly towards the center of the branches. Then, by some miracle, it continued to climb—directly over the apex of the tree, before curving towards the middle of the fairway about 80 yards from the green. Walking to my ball, I felt quite detached from the shot in front of me, yet completely confident that a 54-degree wedge would be the perfect approach. I then knocked the ball right at the pin and it came to rest 7 or so feet directly behind the hole. I left my birdie putt on the edge and tapped in for par and a 38.

The Sensei and I rejoiced near the clubhouse, hugged again in the parking lot, and said goodbye. When I returned home, I was glowing like a pregnant woman. My wife was sufficiently surprised by my remarkable level of relaxation and bonhomie that she was more than willing to look past the fact that I discussed my 38 at dinner with her parents as if it were an event equal to her birth.

But, it didn't stop there. I went out to Wilmette a few days later and shot an 81: 39 on the front, 42 on the back. Then I did the same at Winnetka: 40/41. There were some 82s. In all I broke 40 at least five times over the next eight rounds I played.

Somehow, the new me on the golf course was crossing over into my personal life. I hadn't been so relaxed since my college years. My anxieties eased and flew by like puffy clouds.

Maybe the best example of my equanimity came while on a week-long vacation in Michigan during late August. Renting a house near the beach, we swam and ate and went on dune buggy rides. My father-in-law came for a visit. I played nine holes of spectacular 2-over golf at a place called Hawkshead. Everyone was having a blast.

Then, on a boring afternoon, we decided to visit a combination petting zoo/amusement park about twenty minutes from the house we were renting. I will not name the place, but can tell you that it had been maintained in a fashion that seemed to pay little attention to minor details, like the health of the animals (all of whom seemed to have some variant of pinkeye), the smells that were being emitted, and the maintenance of pretty much any equipment. The completely random and bizarre nature of the place was underscored by a cigar store Indian in a Milwaukee Braves #44 jersey that greeted visitors at the ticket window. When I asked the owner about why and how they acquired a large wooden Hank Aaron, she responded, "Who's Hank Aaron?"

After an hour or so of petting llamas who appeared to be molting out of season and eating suspect snow cones, my five-year-old, Leo, decided it was time to go on some of the rides, all of which were operated by a chain-smoking, toothless woman in her late sixties. Because there was only one operator for six rides, everyone lined up at a single ride, which the woman would operate for five minutes, then lead us all to the next and the next, until we finally arrived at the Ferris wheel, which required an adult to sit with any child under 80 pounds. I volunteered.

My first tipoff that something was a bit off kilter came when the toothless woman asked the parent and child in front of us to get on the wheel, and asked their weights. We were next, and again she asked how much we weighed. Quickly doing some kind of calculation in her head she rotated the wheel three eighths of a revolution and had us climb in a buggy. This continued, everyone seated in some random pattern by size until she apparently was confident that the wheel was unlikely to tip over.

In days past, I would have asked to get off or—if feeling particularly brave—might have just squeezed my eyes shut and envisioned my imminent death over and over until the ride was complete. And, if you think I was perhaps overreacting, my wife, a classic Irish Catholic worrier about nothing (death is apparently a promotion in her culture), said that she began making plans for life as a single mother of three as she watched the two of us.

The reason for her fear was simple. The wheel went at variable speeds. It would move very, very slowly, then suddenly speed up dramatically at random intervals. In fact, there were moments where I tried to decide if I'd ever been on a roller coaster this fast.

But, somehow, as the big wheel creaked and groaned, I looked at my son, who was having a ball, and decided that I should join him. I also thought that if I was going to die young, there were worse ways to go than tumbling through the Michigan pines on a runaway amusement park ride. Even if I were merely crippled, I reasoned, it would make a great story. So, I raised my hands off the safety bar and laughed with my son Leo for everything I was worth.

o o o o

A week after we returned from vacation, my kids started school in a new district.

That first day, I dropped them off, grabbed a coffee, and wrote at Starbucks for two hours; then, at about 11:00, I headed to Winnetka. Knowing that my wife was busy I left her a voice mail explaining that I'd gotten a lot of work done and was going to just play a quick eighteen.

I was at even par and walking up the fifth fairway when she called me back.

"There is only one way that I'm not going to kill you," she said, "and that's if you promise to pick up William from school at 3:15."

"Not a problem," I told her. I figured that the course was wide open and that no matter how well I was playing, I was centered and capable enough of leaving a few holes early if need be.

I finished the front with a 3-over 38.

On the back I had to pair up with a middle-aged accountant and a man in his nineties who had an oxygen tank in his cart. This slowed things up considerably, but I didn't care. It was a great day, I was playing well, and all was right in the world.

I had a few bogeys and a double, but also several pars. By fifteen, I realized that I was in the neighborhood where I might break 80 for the first time. It was 2:30. I explained to the accountant that I was probably going to bail after sixteen.

"Are you out of your mind?" he asked. "I saw your card. You had a 38 on the front and you might break 80. Have you? Ever?"

I admitted that I hadn't. But, yes, ironically, I was having the round of my life, which was made possible by two things: 1) the understanding that I might never be able to finish the round of my life and 2) the fact that I was not thinking about the fact that this was the round of my life.

I parred sixteen and bogeyed seventeen. It was 3:01. If I birdied the 440-yard par-4 eighteenth, I'd shoot 79. It seemed ridiculous to even consider it.

"I'm just going to hit my drive," I explained. "And then I might just pick up."

I nailed one, 260 or so down the left side of the fairway.

"I'm just going to hit my approach and pick up," I explained this time.

It was 3:05.

My 4-hybrid landed 20 yards short and left of the green.

I looked around, panting like a maniac, grabbed a wedge, took a half-swing, landing the ball a few feet past the apron of the green and watched it roll directly at the hole, where it came to rest 8 inches from the cup. I was in at 42 for an 80.

It was 3:09. I grabbed my ball, screamed goodbye, and ran across the parking lot. Tossing my clubs in the back seat, I drove like an idiot, winding through the forest preserve and into the pickup area at West School, arriving at 3:14.

Relieved, I got out to say hi to William's teacher. After a minute I looked down and realized that I was still wearing my golf shoes.

o o o o

My stellar play continued. My bad rounds were between 85 and 87, but mostly there were lots of 81s and 82s. All seemed right with the world.

Then, in early September, Abbot John sent me a link to some essays about Zen ox-herding pictures, which serve as an allegory for the spiritual journey towards enlightenment.

Over the years, there have been many different drawings of this series and just as many, if not more, interpretations. In this way Buddhism is a nice parallel to the old joke in which a sage rabbi is asked for the meaning of life. He strokes his beard and a thoughtful look crosses his face. "Life is like a bowl of cherries," the rabbi tells his student. A few days later, the student returns and says, "I don't understand how life is like a bowl of cherries." The rabbi—like my father discussing heaven—shrugs his shoulders and responds, "So maybe it's not like a bowl of cherries."

That is what I thought of when I first saw that in some versions of this instructive tale there were eight pictures and in others there were ten. In some, the ox changes from black to white—and in some he does not. In some, the final frame shows the ox herder—or perhaps another individual—as drunk. Meanwhile, in others, the herder, the ox, and all disappear.

The basic arc of the story, however, is pretty much the same. It begins with some form of search for or struggle with the ox. This demonstrates that the herder has begun to seek out deeper meaning in his life. When he discovers the ox's footprints, he now sees that there is a path. Seeing the ox—which represents his mind—he then attempts to tame it. This involves a great struggle, but eventually he has turned the animal around and joyfully rides it home. Soon his mind is clear and at peace.

I prefer the final frame that depicts the empty circle of nothingness and unity. There is too much disagreement about the drunk ending, and having spent my late teens and early twenties in a fairly constant state of inebriation, I don't recall any deep sense of peace, except for the summer I drank a pitcher of gin and tonics every night.

The ox-herding series came to me at the right time. It allowed me to assess where I was on my journey towards self-mastery on and off the course. My handicap was now an 11.8, down just over six strokes. I was playing the best golf of my life and feeling ready to break through in every possible way.

I also realized that I was not yet riding my ox home, nor had I been subsumed into a circle of total unity. In an attempt to be honest with myself, I looked at the herding pictures again and again. I had begun the search, found the path, seen the ox, caught it, and was probably getting fairly well along in the process of taming the beast and turning it around.

Historically, this would be a moment where I'd quit. I'm a great half-doer of things. Yet, on every level I knew that I needed to go all the way. I needed to finally be done with my damn ego, but also realized that my ego was certainly not yet done with me.

To hop up on that ox and ride off into the spiritual sunset toward Crosby-like mellow and a single digit handicap, I needed to do something. Something big. Thus, I began to make plans for a trip I had insisted that I would never make. I needed to take my journey to the most hackneyed, overdone golf pilgrimage destination known to man. It was a journey that had been taken by innumerable well-heeled golfers, both spiritual and secular. It was a journey that had been done to death by every golf writer to ever touch this subject. I was on my way to Scotland, where I hoped to unify my opposites and eat the banana of self-knowledge.

Welcome to the Kingdom

Be happy while ye'r living, fur ye'r a lang time deid.

—OLD SCOTTISH PROVERB

FALL 2008. EDINBURGH, SCOTLAND

As my plane began its descent into Edinburgh, I looked out the window at a landscape both familiar and surprising. I'd been to both Ireland and England; thus I had some preconceived notion that Scotland would be similarly lush, green, wet, and cold. And indeed it was all of those things. But, as I looked at the mountains, the Firth of Forth, and the North Sea, I sensed something different. The land was wild, untamed, and prehistoric; all of it seemed either uncommonly soft or frighteningly jagged; every body of water was beautiful, black, and deep.

My next surprise came at the car rental agency. Having read *Golf in the Kingdom* and having listened to it on tape several times, I'd always been somewhat cynical about characters calling it "gawf" and wondering about playing "the coorse wi' the baffin' spoon." The whole thing smacked of Mike Myers. No one, I suspected, actually spoke that way. Then I got in line to rent a car.

I was standing behind a Frenchman and his wife, who listened intently as a young Scot in a green National Car Rental vest gave them directions. At least that's what I think he was doing, because his voice seemed to be nothing but a blur of "wwww...oooooo...rrrr." For all I knew, he could be explaining how to gut and clean a salmon. I looked down the counter and heard another young Scot giving a similarly incomprehensible explanation to someone else.

When I approached the counter, my ears had adjusted to the point where the two men seemed to be speaking a discernible language of some kind.

"Hi, how are you?" I asked.

"Weel, the sun is oot, which is aye a boonus in Scootlund," he replied cheerily, his translucent white skin a testament to the truth of his statement.

The accent wasn't bullshit. And with each passing day I spent in Scotland, I became certain of one thing above all—it is a country of eminently polite people where nobody is blowing smoke up anyone's ass.

This was reinforced when I took a walk along the very touristy Royal Mile that afternoon where I saw, among other things: someone playing bagpipes; endless shops selling fine Scotch, woolens, and kilts; a man dressed in full-on blue-faced, crazy-haired, William Wallace regalia, handing out flyers; innumerable restaurants offering Cullen Skink and black pudding; a sign that read "Haggis Samosa's Are Back!!!"; and a man who—without irony—was sporting a Rod Stewart–circa-1983 haircut. And somehow, in some intangible way, this all felt authentic and genuine. Though I was as far away as I'd ever been from my wife and kids, it was a place where I felt suddenly—and without reason—quite at home.

o o o o

The following morning I grabbed my golf bag and took a cab to the Murrayfield section of town where I was going to spend the day with Mahadeva Ishaya, a monk of the Ishaya order and an avid golfer.

Though we'd only communicated by email, I had a fairly clear picture of Mahadeva in my mind. He was Indian or South Asian. He had a long, graying beard. He would be dressed in robes, flowing of course, and preferably orange. His voice would be a bit like Apu's from *The Simpsons,* but with a heavy dollop of gravitas. And he would have that look in his dancing, but slightly bewildered, eyes that said he lived in a state of pure bliss, and that signified one thing—GURU.

When the cab arrived at the address I'd been given, I was immediately disappointed and confused. As I had with Yoni, I expected a studio, a driving range, even a house of worship. Instead, I was in a residential neighborhood of gray three-flats.

I rang the bell marked "Ishaya" and a man's voice told me to come up to the third floor. Swinging my clubs past a few bikes in the front hallway, I dragged them up three flights until I arrived at Mahadeva's apartment. And there in the open doorway stood a particularly Scottish-looking white man, with pale skin and a receding brown hairline. The man was wearing a black Slazenger golf shirt and black Dunlop golf pants. As he extended his hand to shake mine, I thought, "This is not my Mahadeva!!!!" But, indeed he was one and the same.

Taking my golf bag, Mahadeva smiled and led me into the kitchen, where he'd made tea for himself and coffee for me. We discussed my flight, the cold, wet forecast for the next few days, and what we'd be doing during my visit.

I was going to go through "First Sphere," the introductory stage of learning the Ishaya Ascension method of meditation. This would take place over two days—with a day in between when I had a golf date with a Scottish poet and a Buddhist window maker. On day one, we would learn the first two "attitudes" in the morning and then, weather permitting, we'd play a bit of golf in the afternoon. Two days later, I would learn attitudes three and four, followed by a round of golf at Gullane, a course on the Firth of Forth and—according to every cab driver I encountered—one of the finest courses in Scotland.

After a few minutes, Mahadeva invited me upstairs, which meant climbing a ladder through the ceiling into a small solarium perched on the roof of his building. As the trap door closed behind us, I became of two minds, or maybe three.

The peaceful half of my mind marveled at the room. It was lovely, with amazing views in all directions. On clear days, you could look across the rooftops and see the Firth of Forth.

The other side of my brain, however, was divided in half. One quarter was observing the other quarter in an altogether detached and meditative manner. Which was good, because the other portion, which contains my cowering inner Don Knotts, was freaking the fuck out. Here I was, across the Atlantic, at the apartment of a complete stranger (once again whom I'd found on the Internet)—and I have just crawled through a trap door in the ceiling into a small space completely removed from the rest of humanity. That part of me was looking at the cup of coffee, from which I'd barely taken more than a sip, and thinking over and over, "So this is how it all ends. I drink the poisoned coffee, I get very sleepy, and I am then semi-conscious but unable to move while I am eaten by a depraved Scottish Idi Amin, my blood spattering the windows of this lovely solarium where no one can see the carnage."

Sitting on a futon sofa and scribbling unintelligible notes, I stared at the cup of coffee, in the well-developed part of my brain that handles the flight portion of my "fight or flight" panic response. I began dreaming up a context in which I might be able to drop a hint that there was someone who would be expecting me at some point, someone who would know something was amiss if I didn't return uneaten to the Scotsman Hotel downtown by dinner that evening—anything that might prevent my being choked with a karate belt and torn asunder before I'd even reached the age of forty-two. My wife, I thought. That's it! "My wife." I decided that she was—at this very moment—at the hotel (rather than in Chicago), waiting to have lunch or dinner, or better yet, WAITING FOR A PHONE CALL!!! "Yes," I thought, "I'll pull the phone from my pocket and say, 'This is in case my wife calls FROM THE HOTEL—WHERE SHE IS WAITING FOR ME!!!'"

But I didn't. Instead, I looked at Mahadeva and realized that this was about me, not him. He seemed like a wonderful guy who was giving me his time, expertise, and, quite frankly, his caring sense that I was worthy of his assistance. And in some bizarre testament to how far I'd come on this journey, I was able to tell myself with reasonable certainty that this was a kind, considerate man with no taste for human flesh.

I took a swig of my coffee and bravely pressed on.

o o o o

Mahadeva is forty-five and a Glaswegian who came to Edinburgh for school and never left. He is a former atheist who went through a period of being very, very angry—at himself, others, and the world. That was during his teens and twenties, when his parents divorced and most young men, even the well-adjusted (whoever they are), need to blow off a lot of steam.

Sitting there across from Mahadeva in this room, it is difficult to believe that he was ever angry. He is soft-spoken, thoughtful, and very gentle in his demeanor. As we talk, I realize that in addition to our love of golf and interest in Eastern spirituality, we both have tangled with the essential problem of feeling inadequate on some level. And for this we have both punished ourselves, something I do by concocting scenarios in which I'm dying. As he speaks, I think that my anxiety is not so unlike that of a retired deli owner whose daughter said that he still came into work in case there was a crisis. And when there wasn't a crisis, he created one.

In dribs and drabs, however, I have begun to shed that side of myself. The anxiety attacks are fewer and farther between and their intensity has diminished with more frequent meditation and in some perverse way with the improvement in my golf game. But still I wanted more. I wanted the whole ball of wax, and as best I could tell, Ishaya Ascension was a valid avenue to nirvana.

At least that's how it sounds when you read the words of its founder, R. Vaughn Abrams, an American who came to be known as MSI—Maharishi Sadashiva Isharn. MSI believed that life was "meant to be lived in eternal joy, infinite freedom, unconditional love, and unbounded awareness," all of which are much more than I had ever hoped for. I'd come for the relief of stress and anxiety, but was more than willing to partake of the infinite freedom, unconditional love, and awareness.

About a decade before, Mahadeva had been dealing with his stress and anger via yoga and meditation, the latter of which he did in such diligent Scottish-Presbyterian fashion that it would often result in blinding headaches. Then a friend introduced him to Ascension, which Mahadeva studied for six months in Canada before teaching in Mexico and returning to Scotland with two primary urges: 1) to teach Ascension and 2) to play some golf, which led to Golf in the Moment—mental game instruction based in the Ishaya method.

Golf, Mahadeva realized, was a terrific metaphor for life, or at the very least a place where our best and worst selves are on display.

"I saw the chaos in my head and how it manifested itself on the course. It was this huge battle. . . . There is no place I was more likely to lose it than while I was playing golf. There was something there for me to investigate," he told me as we sat in the solarium.

Golf, however, would have to wait until the afternoon, because that morning we were going to investigate the inside of my head using the Ishaya "attitudes" of praise and gratitude. These emotions, combined with the attitudes of love and compassion, were powerful and transformative. Harnessing their power was the key to freeing my mind.

Sitting on the floor, Mahadeva uses a black marker to draw an infinity sign on a dry-erase board. Infinity (also the centerpiece of the Shivas Irons Society logo) symbolizes "the Ascendant," the mind with which we are born, the pure, innocent spirit of a child who experiences the world without preconceptions, judgments, or hang-ups. The Ascendant is the golden statue before it is covered with mud; it is the little girl in Les Bolland's video, swinging at the ball and not caring if she hits it or not; it's my youngest son at age eleven months, climbing a step ladder and teetering on top with a gigantic smile, thrilled with himself and unafraid that he is about to crack his coconut if he falls. The Ascendant is the metaphysical authentic swing we seek after realizing that all external stimuli fail to give us total fulfillment.

So, the goal is to get to the Ascendant again.

Our mind, however, is like a tree. As we age, rings form around that infinity sign. They are rings of experience—good and bad. These rings become our thoughts and mind chatter, which then circle the authentic self. Thus, all information must travel through those rings before it gains access to our infinite, ascendant nature. And by the time it gets there, those thoughts have been transformed from something pure, clear, and untarnished into some unrecognizable coded message that carries all of our baggage along with it.

Now, it's pretty easy to think that the key to dealing with this situation is to get rid of the thoughts that keep us from our ascendant self. Almost every aspiring meditator begins with the misconception that a breathing practice will banish those thoughts and move them out of the way. And most of us push like hell to get rid of them, which is a big mistake.

"Trying to stop a thought is like trying to stop a wave," Mahadeva tells me. "It just creates another wave."

Instead, he tells me that thoughts, if left alone, will move. The problem is when we grab onto them. He illustrates this for me by saying that if we stand in the middle of a busy street, most of our effort will be dedicated to avoiding cars. But if we are on the sidewalk observing the traffic, we are out of danger. The bottom line is that we will always have thoughts. Yet, if we acknowledge their presence and remain detached, they will pass. Via Ascension I was about to learn how to pull myself out of traffic and onto the sidewalk where I belong.

o o o o

We begin by selecting my "star word," a word that I will use in practicing Ascension by inserting it mantra-like into four sentences, each representing one of the attitudes. I choose "life" and we begin with praise. Because, according to Mahadeva, using these attitudes cuts through the rings around our infinity sign by integrating both hemispheres of the brain (the analytical, masculine left and the creative, emotional right) and making them work together, which magically gives the brain what it seeks and puts us in a mental space of being present and alive.

Mahadeva makes me promise to not divulge the exact wording of the mantras, but suffice to say, I am giving praise to life. Thus, I sit on the sofa in a meditative posture, breathing in and out as I normally would. Then, when the mood strikes, I praise life in a very specific manner, repeating the phrase whenever I feel the urge, be it every four seconds or every four minutes.

Unlike a mantra, there was a fluid quality to using the attitude of praise. For reasons I can't explain, I seemed to know when to use it and when to simply observe my thoughts. And amazingly, whenever I did praise life, it would dissolve any thought to which I'd become attached.

Now, it may be that I am away from home and the ever present whir of four kids, three dogs attempting to kill the cat, and never-ending screams of "I want that" every time there is a commercial on Cartoon Network, but I begin to experience things differently. I feel completely without purpose in my breathing, which somehow has put me very much in sync with that very same breath. I zone out for periods of time, yet I never beat myself up when I return. Instead, it's back to the breathing and praising life whenever I want. I begin to have the inkling that I am feeling what meditation is actually all about.

Mahadeva very quietly asks me to open my eyes. I ask him how long I've been meditating. He tells me he has no idea. A quick look at my watch and I guess to myself that it was well over thirty minutes.

Then we shift to gratitude, and Mahadeva asks me to begin my meditation by counting my thoughts for a few minutes before inserting my star word into a sentence that gives thanks to life. And this is where it gets very interesting.

Sitting and breathing, I get perhaps the first glimpse of the way my mind works at a deeper level, underneath the nervous chatter. Here is a rough idea of how it went. For the first forty-five seconds or so, my mind was blank. There were no thoughts for me to count. Then I started thinking about how clear my mind was and wondering if that was a thought in and of itself. This gave way to my golf game, how I might play that afternoon, how good a golfer Mahadeva was, and could I keep my drives in the fairway? As those thoughts drifted from my consciousness I began wondering what Mahadeva was doing while I meditated. Was he meditating himself? Or was he watching me? Should I open my eyes and check? But what if he was watching me? Before long, I began thinking about lunch and then, inexplicably, I ran smack dab into Kelly Ripa. There was nothing in particular about her filling my mind, only the fact of her mere existence. The thought was simply "Kelly Ripa," in the same way you think "It's really dark tonight." No judgment, no reason, just a thought.

This continued for a minute or two. I began to see patterns and the thoughts behind my thoughts. Then Mahadeva told me to stop counting and to start meditating as I had before but adding the gratitude mantra.

When it was over, we discussed the nature of thoughts.

"When we believe our thoughts," Mahadeva tells me, "we forget what we are."

o o o o

After a lunch of carrot soup, brown bread, and cheese, Mahadeva and I look out his kitchen window. It has been dark all day and rained a bit, but nothing that will preclude golf. So, we pack up our bags and head to Braid Hills, where we play the nine-hole Princes course, which sit adjacent to Braid's full eighteen, where I will be playing the next day.

We both have our good and bad holes. But there are two important moments. The first is when Mahadeva tells me to look at the horizon. From this vantage point, I can see downtown Edinburgh, where a dark sky hangs over the old part of town, which looks like a stone fortress that rises from the more modern portions of the city. To the left, a full, shimmering rainbow hangs over the water, as the sun shines through a haze. The contrast is breathtaking.

The other moment is on the fourth hole, when Mahadeva tells me about shooting his career-best 84 not long ago and wondering to himself, "What if this is the best round that I ever play?"

The question hangs there for a moment. Mahadeva smiles, at peace with the idea. I have no response to a thought so terrifying.

o o o o

After finishing up on the par-3 ninth, Mahadeva and I grabbed a cup of hot chocolate in the clubhouse and then he drove me back to my hotel. It was now dark, and he got out of the car while I grabbed my clubs from the back.

For our next meeting, he told me that there would be a *puja* ceremony to mark my completion of first sphere. To fulfill my end of the bargain, he said that I should bring six or eight cut flowers and three pieces of whole sweet fruit, which I dutifully wrote in my notebook.

Then Mahadeva approached me, held out his arms, and hugged me, before getting in his car, leaving me standing with my golf clubs, in the dark, on a cold, wet street in downtown Edinburgh.

o o o o

I first found out about Andrew Greig from Printer Bowler, who said that there was a Scottish poet who'd nearly died from an unexpected brain aneurysm and then wrote a book about recouping his health and life on the golf courses of Scotland.

At first I thought little of it, other than to order a copy of *Preferred Lies* from Amazon. I read the book in bits and pieces over the course of several months and became more and more convinced that I ought to at least contact Greig to see if he would be in the United States at any point during the following year and—if so—whether he'd be up for playing some golf with me.

In our correspondence he was welcoming, enthusiastic (within the context of being Scottish), and intrigued by what I was doing. A trip to the States, however, was not in his plans. But if I came to Scotland, he'd happily play eighteen with me at Braid.

The more I read his book, the more I thought it might be important for me to visit the cradle of the game. Greig's writing was poetic—as one might expect—but somehow unsentimental in a lyrical sort of way. It seemed that he understood the game and its spiritual nature on a deep level that cut through the crap and saw golf for what it was and what it wasn't.

"Golf isn't life," he had written. "It's just a small radiant corner of it, like a chip of mirror-glass, the kind where if you bring it close enough and examine it carefully from a number of angles, you can see the whole of your eye, and a surprising amount of the world around you."

I'm not sure if it was his close brush with death or his take on the game that made me decide to make the trip, but by late August, it seemed as if there was an irresistible force drawing me to him, Mahadeva, and the holy land. I wasn't sure what I would gain from my time with Andrew, but I had sufficient faith to land on his doorstep around noon on a cool, misty day in early October 2008.

o o o o

Andrew Greig greets me at his front door. Solidly built, handsome, and in his mid-fifties, he doesn't look like someone who almost died as much as he seems like a scholarly former mountain climber (which he is) who has decided that waking up in the morning, getting paid to write, and playing a bit of golf is as much excitement as he requires from life.

After we shake hands, I notice his eyes drifting to the lightweight Titliest golf bag purchased earlier in the year because it was easy to carry through airports and had fewer than forty-seven pockets.

"Well," he says seriously, "that's an admirably modest bag."

In the moment, I felt a bit self-conscious. I knew he wasn't tooling on me, but I had that feeling of being found out, like when you wear a jersey and somebody says, "So, you're a big White Sox fan, huh?" And yes, you are. And yes, that's why you bought and are wearing the jersey, but you can't help feeling a little exposed somehow.

It was only later that day when I would come to realize that praise of modesty is about as big a compliment as anyone dishes out on this island.

Inside Andrew's house it is warm. He leads me to the kitchen, where he is preparing a lunch similar to what Mahadeva served the day before. Soup, bread, butter, and cheese. Standing there, I do the socio-culinary math and reason that there can't be many

Jews in a country with so much soup, none of it containing a large, unyielding mass at its center or serving as a prelude to shrimp toast and Mongolian Beef.

Then Vin enters the room.

Vin Harris runs Fairways to Heaven, a decidedly unprofitable, but highly enjoyable venture that arranges four- to six-day spiritual golf tours that include meditation, club throwing, and hitting balls into the ocean. It was somewhere during the second half of his journey that someone had told Andrew, "I've a friend you should meet. He combines your main interests—golf, mindfulness, and death! Vin is a golfing, Tibetan Buddhist undertaker."

As it turns out, the undertaker part is only half true, in that Vin is a window maker who does coffins on the side. But, he is also the real deal, an Englishman who came to Scotland over thirty years ago to help build the Samye Ling Tibetan Buddhist monastery in Dumfriesshire. He's been to Tibet, he's a practicing Buddhist, and, after taking up golf at forty, he is a good player who isn't at the top of his game when we get together.

Vin is one of the first people I've met whose energy changes a room—making everyone in it more relaxed. He is a conventional enough looking man of the British Isles, with gray hair and the flushed red cheeks of someone who spends time outdoors in all kinds of weather. But there is something altogether different about him that emanates from a mouth that is bent into a perpetual smile and eyes that are as alive with both mischief and chi as any I've ever seen.

As we eat in the living room someone brings up the 2008 Ryder Cup, in which the Americans broke a long drought and won an emotional victory over Nick Faldo's Europeans. I sit there amazed as both Andrew and Vin agree that they were happy about the result.

"It used to be that the Europeans were the interesting team—the team that had a personality—and the Americans were like robots," Vin says. "But, now, it's the other way around. The Americans were easy to cheer for."

This conversation gives way to both of them wondering what exactly I'm doing in writing this book and why I am here. Andrew says that he's read something online where it was described as being about "golf, spirituality, and—do I have this right?—concepts of American manhood or something like that."

I tell them that I had begun the project attempting to reconcile a world in which God, Buddha, and Bhagavad collided with Pat Summerall, Ken Venturi, and Johnny Miller. Yet, along the way, that weird marriage seemed to matter less and less. The connection no longer seemed quite so esoteric or ridiculous. Instead, I was beginning to feel less and less like an outsider in this golf-and-spirituality world. What I didn't explain, however, was my fear that, like Colonel Kurtz in *Heart of Darkness/Apocalypse Now*, I had crossed over to the other side and was going native.

After we clear the dishes, Andrew brings in some tea and talk turns to the American tendency to believe that the most important element of one's game is the ability to hit 300-yard drives.

"Right," Vin says, his eyes laughing. "Kill the ball. Hit the shit out of it."

I confess that even I, the freshly minted Ascender, can fall prey to such pedestrian wants and delusions.

o o o o

Thirty minutes later, we are on the first tee at Braid Hills, bundled up against the gray sky and temperatures in the low 50s. Each day of this trip, I pick up the paper and the forecast is for frigid weather and pouring rain. But somehow, each day the rain seems to confine itself to the evenings, causing everyone I meet to say, "Ye brought th' waither wi' you."

I refrain from noting that none of them appear to have ever visited Chicago.

Andrew tees off first. His swing is flat, even, and powerful, made even more so by a last minute hitch in the wrists as his club wraps around his body on the way back. His movements are economical and, even though he is fifteen years my senior, he outdrives me by 20 to 30 yards on nearly every hole.

The first hole is my real introduction to Scottish golf. It's an uphill par-4. By this, I don't mean uphill in any conventional sense. It's not "It's uphill." Nor is it "Add a club because it's uphill." Not even "It's uphill, then there is an elevated green." None of those do justice to the terrifying steepness of the first hole at Braid. If there were a club longer than a driver, I would say it was a four-club hill, large enough that you are hitting a blind tee shot in which the ball disappears after about 50 yards. And it's into the wind.

Andrew's ball is long and towards the right edge of the fairway—if any of us could actually see the fairway.

Vin tees up his ball and waggles a bit. His swing is somewhat opposite of Andrew's. It is long, fluid, and relaxed. Though he took up golf in his forties, he is graceful and unforced in a way that often eludes those who don't play until after they reach thirty. And while he isn't powerful, Vin's ball flies long enough and very straight. There is a noticeable lack of teeth-grinding each time he stands over a ball.

With a smooth swish back and forth, he pops one toward Andrew's ball but a bit shorter and closer to the center of the fairway.

Then I step up. I take a few practice swings and lean over my ball. I breathe in and out a few times, then begin my backswing.

"Kill it, Josh!" Vin screams to me. "Really hit the fucking shit out of it."

Well, I suppose that you just haven't been on a spiritual golf quest until a Buddhist has yelled something like that. I look back and laugh, then pull a decent drive down the left side, landing just off the edge of the fairway in the rough.

When I get to my ball, I see that there is a sharp drop left of the green and hitting over looks pretty dicey. Thus, I aim for the right side where it looks safe. I'm about 110 yards out, but the wind is very strong. So I pull out my 8–iron and hit a majestic, high shot that is perfect, but headed for the left edge. The greens, I will come to find, are hard as rocks and everything runs like crazy. Eventually, it will get through my head that I must bump and run, but on this shot, the ball drops like an anvil and sticks on the back left about 12 feet past the hole and 5 feet from running off.

Vin and Andrew also get on in regulation and as we walk up the fairway I am filled with utter confidence that I will drop my putt. When I reach my ball, I bend my knees and see that it breaks slightly left to right before I stand, take a deep breath, and knock it in the center of the hole for a birdie.

As we walk off, Vin gives me a look.

"Easy fucking game," I say as we head to the second.

"I know," he responds. "Can you believe that people write books about this shit?"

It was the last time I would have that feeling at Braid Hills. The rest of the front nine and part of the back were marked by bogeys, doubles, and a par or two. Andrew and Vin were up and down as well, but we rooted for each other on our good holes and laughed at the bad.

At the par-3 ninth, Andrew suggests that we play a silent hole in which no one speaks from the time the first ball is struck until the last man has holed his putt. The quiet gives me a chance to look around at what is a remarkable landscape. Braid Hills is ancient—and though someone obviously took the time to design it as a golf course, it seems as if the course itself is part of the natural topography. It's a parkland—rather than links style— layout, but that can hardly describe the way the holes seem to run in and out of canyons, down cliffs, and up high over the city. Though I tend to like the way that golf courses look and obviously have more than a passing interest in the game, I have always tried to maintain some perspective on the fact that a golf course is, in fact, man-made and not a majestic, natural miracle that is all part of God's grand plan. At Braid Hills, that changes on the back nine.

The one hole that I recall most vividly is a narrow hollow that has been cut into the hill by some divine force and whose fairway feels like a river spilling naturally towards the putting surface It is as natural and beautiful a place as I have ever been to in my life. Having scrupulously avoided "nature" for decades, I am dumbstruck by how in touch with it I suddenly feel. This sense stays with me until I am on another hole, where the nearly black sky hangs over me on the fairway, but just behind the green I can see that there is a seam in the clouds where a gigantic shaft of light beams downwards with an intensity I have never before seen. A lifelong agnostic, I stop and look at it for quite a long time. If ever there was a moment in my life that I knew there was a God—this is it.

The most stunning of all, however, was the weather and how it played out across the sky. On nearly every hole it took my breath away. At one moment you could be standing in the sunlight and look outwards to see a full rainbow in one direction and charcoal skies dropping sheets of rain in another.

With great finality, I suddenly understood why people come here and why it's not just another golf vacation.

o o o o

Shortly after we make the turn, Andrew confesses that he's been admiring my driver and I explain that it's a Taylor-Made Burner with a draw bias, which has been doing a nice job of keeping me closer to the fairway on days when I am a bit wild off the tee.

On the next hole, he breaks down and asks if he can try it. I hand him the club and he takes several practice cuts, getting used to its weight and length before he tees up his ball.

Andrew's issues off the tee are the opposite of mine. He has the high-class golfer's problem of hooking when his swing isn't going right. But, as Les Bolland told me, that is the right problem to have. All of the great ones—Hogan being the prime example—tangled with a hook at some point before mastering their swing.

So, as he stands there, I worry that Andrew is going to hit a ball that starts curving left and never stops. But I am wrong. He gets up and takes a giant cut, with a swing far faster than any he's uncorked that day. The ball starts right and keeps on going further and further right until it becomes clear that he ought to hit another one with his own driver.

"Fucking thing doesn't work," he says, handing the club back to me.

A hole or two later, I come to realize the folly of my approach to golf in Scotland, and my connection to the course deepens. I had come here under the impression that my game was what mattered, and that I could make the world somehow bend to it. Thus, for the better part of twenty-three holes over the last two days, I have swung for the greens and put my ball in the air on everything but chips, completely oblivious to the reality of the course. This comes into greater focus when I am 140 yards from the green and about to hit a 7-iron. To my right on the fairway, Vin notices that I am pausing longer than usual.

"I don't mean this in a flakey way," he says, "but sometimes the contours of the hole are talking to you. And you just have to listen."

I put my 7-iron back into my bag, realizing that hitting the ball high into the wind and trying to stick iron shots onto greens where everything runs off are not strategies that serve me well on this island. There is a visceral way in which I feel what Vin is describing. It's like relaxing into the earth with your feet and your mind—achieving some kind of unity that tells you what is right, and borders on Chevy Chase putting blindfolded in *Caddyshack*. The hole, actually make that the entire course, is telling me to bump and run. Thus, I grab my 5-iron and with a 2/3 swing hit one that bounces 50 yards before the green and rolls up to 6 feet from the cup.

o o o o

During the entire eighteen holes, Andrew and Vin did not keep score. I did for a while, then abandoned my card as well. Both said that they usually could tally up their holes afterward, but what really mattered were what Andrew called the "loofah moments," those shots and holes that you remember in the shower or the bath. The ones that felt good and that you hope to have more of every time you head to the course.

That said, I heated up a bit on the last few holes, bumping and running everything and using my 5-iron for nearly every shot between 50 and 170 yards. I had a few pars and a bogey or two, but I mostly remember the feel and the sense of unity with the course beneath me.

o o o o

On the way home, we stop at a neighborhood pub to grab a pint and talk. As we stand at the bar, I insist on buying and Andrew highly recommends that I try the India Pale Ale. But I ask for a pint of hard cider instead. This mystifies Andrew, who asks a few more times if that is really what I want, and whether I might reconsider and try the ale, which is quite good. No, I say, I'll have the cider. But as the bartender pours my drink, I suspect that Andrew is trying to politely steer me away from a drink that should only be ordered by someone wearing a dress—or maybe he just really thinks the ale is that good.

Then I leave a tip on the bar. The bartender walks by and makes a strange face. Andrew picks it up, gives the money back to me, and we go to the table where he explains that people don't leave tips for bartenders in Scotland. It is not the last aspect of this pub that I find interesting, because it is a singular representation of the Scottish character—and here's how. I notice that the bar is as crowded as pretty much anyplace you'd go in Ireland. There is also just as much alcohol flowing as there would be at any watering hole in Dublin. I search my brain for how and why it is different—only to realize that I can hear myself think. In fact, I can also hear what Vin and Andrew are saying without straining in the least. It is a room of heavy drinking, somber individuals having conversations in normal tones. Scotland, I conclude, is one of the most normal, sober places in the world. It is what we think America was in the 50s, but without the segregation. The entire nation is completely without guile.

Andrew himself is a perfect representation of this mindset, a fact of which he is keenly aware. After we both order a second drink, we talk about how whenever Andrew or Vin would tell me "nice shot," I'd say something like "thanks." This, I am assured, is not very Scottish and most decidedly American.

In his book, Andrew wrote about a spiritually inclined, golf-obsessed Californian who responded to that compliment by giving a somewhat lengthy and enthusiastic response. A true Scot, by contrast, can only respond with something like "Dumb luck," or "The wind was at my back." Andrew laughs at the kind of reaction he would have gotten from his father had he ever said "thanks" after a good shot in his youth.

o o o o

An hour or so later, we have dropped off Andrew and I am sitting in the passenger seat of Vin's car. I'm a bit "pissed" as they say here, from the two or so pints of cider I consumed, but mostly I feel supremely relaxed.

It is raining when Vin pulls up in front of my hotel. We say our goodbyes. He and Andrew were as good company as one could hope for on any golf course. The kind of people who make you stop keeping score without even knowing it. People who have learned to celebrate the loofah moments in life and on the course, letting the rest fall away—as it should. I grab my clubs out of Vin's trunk and throw them over my shoulder, then extend my right hand in friendship. Vin smiles impishly and pulls me towards him—and we embrace.

Before I have been in this famously reserved country for seventy-two hours, I have hugged two relative strangers more than I have hugged all of my male cousins combined during the prior forty-two years.

Standing in the rain on the sidewalk, just as I had the night before, I wait for the stoplight to change and realize that they are no longer strangers to me.

o o o o

The next morning, I duck into a convenience store and buy three large navel oranges, then grab a cab, asking the driver to stop at a cart downtown, where I find a bunch of blue and yellow flowers to bring to Mahadeva.

When I arrive, we have our coffee and tea, then proceed upstairs again, where love and compassion are the attitudes that we will practice.

Love, Mahadeva tells me, is the most powerful emotion and both the conscious and subconscious motivator for so many of our actions. We think that if we can just get that job, or look that way, or come into enough money to get us that car, then we will feel loved. We look to others to provide us with love—our children, friends, spouses, and parents. Even perfect strangers (yes, I mean you A-Rod, and no, the Yankee fans will never love you like they love Jeter; heal yourself).

But the key is not to focus on your relationship with others. It is to heal your relationship with life. That will allow you to feel love in all its forms and find peace.

So, I sit for a long, long time. Maybe forty minutes. As long as I have ever meditated in one sitting. The experience is remarkable.

After I have counted thoughts for a few minutes, I sink into a very deep sense of awareness. The experience is surreal. I easily move further and further beneath my thoughts, down level after level, until I am no longer having thoughts, but am instead seeing vivid colors that shift shape and size. Yes, it sounds weird. And yes, I sound insane. But, I have to say—it's the truth and I have never felt so at peace.

When we are done, I feel as well rested, relaxed, and happy as I can recall.

Mahadeva tells me that twenty minutes of this kind of peace can be as restful as a night's sleep. And I would have a hard time arguing with that.

Then comes compassion, and eventually I begin using all four attitudes during a single session—in order, and usually in some kind of mathematical rhythm—such as praise, praise, gratitude, love, love, compassion.

When we are done, I still feel great. I am not sure that I am on the doorstep of "ultimate, unified ascendant consciousness," or "exalted ascendant consciousness," but I must say I felt more peaceful and present than I could recall, with a sense of mental clarity with which I was wholly unfamiliar.

As we descend the ladder, I become giddy with anticipation of how this will impact my round at Gullane that afternoon.

o o o o

Before we could leave, Mahadeva asked me for the fruit and flowers, which we took into his bedroom for the puja ceremony—a Buddhist and Hindu offering of thanks to the gods.

Now, as much as I love Mahadeva and as much as I was feeling so at peace and everything, I was initially a bit freaked out. First, I was in the bedroom Mahadeva shares with his wife. And as an adult, something just feels a bit weird to me about being alone in such an intimate place with a stranger—even one whom I've hugged less than forty-eight hours before. Second, even though the Ishaya tradition is nondenominational, I see a picture of Jesus on the table where Mahadeva lays the fruit and flowers as an offering.

Standing with my eyes closed while Mahadeva chanted in Sanskrit, I considered the picture of Christ. My first thought was that I told at least three jokes about Christ during our first meeting, assuming that I was in the company of a Buddhist who believed that the traditional Western religions were a bunch of silliness. I also recalled one of those jokes being one by Bill Maher or George Carlin about not being able to really get down with any religion that revolved around "an imaginary friend."

So that was a bit worrisome. The other side of this was my inner Jew. The one that has no interest in actually being Jewish, but still can't accept Christ as his personal savior. Truth be told, I love going to church with my wife—even funerals. I find

Catholic services soothing on some level that I have never experienced in Judaism. But, that said, I am just Jewish enough to never get over the Christ thing. I mean, definitely a good guy, definitely worth listening to—but not someone I can accept as my personal savior. That much I learned in Hebrew school.

Anyway, I wasn't exactly at peace during the ceremony. In fact, I was really nervous about Christ, the bedroom—the whole puja thing and what the fruit and flowers might ultimately be used for.

But, in retrospect, my fears were meaningless. Mahadeva bore me no ill will for my transgressions against Christ and as he chanted, I began to feel touched that someone, a stranger really, was making an offering to a god, his god, any god on my behalf.

o o o o

The actual town of Gullane is as close as I will ever come to being inserted into one of those charming little seaside villages you see in British films about small town life. You know, the ones where everyone in town is some kind of archetypal, semi-crazed, but ultimately delightful eccentric whose common sense borders on genius.

Before we headed to the course, Mahadeva and I stopped in at a pub for lunch. Peat was burning in the fireplace. Dogs slept on the floor while their owners ate savory pies, drank Guinnesses, and smoked pipes. I sat down, ordered lunch, and was overcome by the thought, "This just can't be real." But it was, giving me a warm, secure feeling when I arrived on the first tee at Gullane No. 2.

Mahadeva and I both hit long, straight drives on the par-4 first hole. The sky overhead was as dark as it had ever been during the trip, but not a drop of rain was falling.

Brimming with confidence and having seen colors that morning while examining the deepest levels of my consciousness, I pulled my 8-iron from my bag, stood over my ball and promptly shanked a shot for the first time in six weeks, landing in some very tall, very unpleasant grass to the right. I was lucky to double. Mahadeva had a very conventional two-putt par.

The front nine was an interesting exercise in staying calm and managing to enjoy watching dramatic weather in the distance on a golf course that was as beautiful, if not more so, than Braid.

Taking in views of the Firth of Forth—and gigantic storms in the distance over Edinburgh and moving across the water in various directions—I was convinced that this was now the second most beautiful place that I'd been in my life. Which may have been a bit of golfing Stockholm syndrome on my part, but it was staggering just the same.

My game was spotty. I had a hard time doing much of anything right for the first seven or so holes. I didn't blow up, but I had one par, mixed with bogeys and doubles. I also had the opportunity to play a par-4 of under 260 yards which made the first at Braid seem like a bunny hill. My cabbie that morning had referred to it as being the "cardiac hole." I laughed. But, when I got to the top of the hill to look for my second shot, I stood there for over a minute, wanting to say something to Mahadeva, but unable to summon sufficient breath to do much more than go: "I'm ... I'm ... ver ... ver ... very ... out ... of ... breath."

It seemed some miracle that the ground wasn't littered with the dead bodies of those who had come before me.

Like a fool, particularly a fool who believed he was just a few meditation sessions away from inner peace and a 6-stroke reduction in his handicap, I had forgotten about bump and run. Instead, I let it all hang out, hitting full 9-irons into the wind, unaware that I was even doing so.

Then on number eight, I came to my senses and got on in regulation with the old bump and run and three-putted for a bogey, which was followed by a similar strategy that led to par on nine, bringing me in at 47 on the front.

My game settled down. My mind calmed. And I began to eat up the back. Mahadeva, who'd been terrific during the first seven, seemed to be falling apart while I got better. Where he'd been calming me on the front, I was now soothing him on the back, telling him to just be calm and let the game come back to him.

We played several holes that bent around the water. The weather continued to provide a dramatic backdrop, and we could see storms heading directly towards us, then veering off and heading back out over the Firth of Forth.

My game continued to be steady and sometimes spectacular. After hitting way right on the fourteenth, I smashed a 3-wood uphill 210 yards and rolled off the back of the green, from which I chipped close and dropped my putt for par.

I was 2 over on the back heading into the sixteenth, a 527-yard par-5. I crushed my drive, as the rain began to fall and the sky turned dark as night. I was in the middle and Mahadeva to the right and 30 yards short of what may have been the longest ball I'd hit off a tee all year. I pulled out my 3-wood, which I'd been deadly with for the past seven holes, and hit a liner into a huge line of bunkers. I decided that I had a good enough lie to hit a hybrid, and hit my third shot into a bunker 100 yards further toward the hole. By the time I hit my last putt, I was 5-over for the back.

I bogeyed the seventeenth and parred the eighteenth as we began to get soaked. In my memory, Mahadeva and I are standing on the eighteenth, the sky is black, there is lightning flashing, and the skies have opened into torrential rains of biblical proportions. I'm guessing it was somehow less dramatic, but just the same, it was finally raining too hard for us to play, just as I'd completed the last of my forty-five holes in Scotland.

Later that night Mahadeva dropped me off as he had two evenings ago and again we hugged on the street. I thanked him profusely and he drove away.

o o o o

As I pack the next morning, I turn on the BBC, which is broad-casting an omen that can only mean that I am getting out before my fantasy of Scotland bursts. That omen comes in the form of back-to-back episodes of *Quincy*, followed by a very special epi-sode of *One Tree Hill*.

I'm not terribly Zen as I weave through Edinburgh traf-fic and construction, losing my way several times on the way to the airport. I curse the GPS, the tram project (that nobody wants, according to one golfing cabbie I met), and scream at a bicyclist with my windows closed. I see the clock ticking further and further towards my departure time. I am upset, angry, and worried—then I remember that these are thoughts. And I also remember something Andrew wrote about the nature of existence.

"Life is worth getting upset about . . . because it's also worth getting happy about. What's the point of getting to the end, and all you can say is: Well, at least it hasn't bothered me much?"

I realize that in some ways this has been my end goal—to not let life bother me too much. Thus, I accept that I am pissed off and frustrated; then I calm down considerably and make my way to the airport, where I arrive late, but still make my flight.

As my flight takes off, I notice something quite unexpected. For the first time in about fifteen years, I am having not a twinge of anxiety about flying. I am not simply managing it, telling myself not to worry, or convincing myself that the odds of a crash are less than those of death by bus or in my own bathroom. Instead, I only think of how good it feels to be climbing upwards, watching the beautiful countryside beneath me. The sound of the engines roaring beneath my feet and every bump and bounce comfort rather than terrify me. I feel warm, secure, and can't wait to get home to my family.

I came to this country with some vague sense of it being part of my quest. I meditated with Mahadeva and saw the wizard behind the curtain in my brain—even if only for a few moments. I played with Vin and Andrew as some method of exorcising my fear of death, asking them not a single question, but simply partaking of the experience. I let go somehow and felt a unity with the turf under my feet. Something inside of me had been cleansed—and I hadn't needed to drink Green Magma to make it happen. For the moment, I had come to terms with the inevitability of my own demise and was living in the moment.

Scotland had done its trick. I felt utterly and completely awake.

The Lost Tribe of Shivas

"I almost disappeared," [Shivas to Michael after going
into a trance]. *"Almost disappeared."*
*A smile formed on his face, spreading slowly as if the muscles around
his mouth had grown stiff. His eyes looked straight into mine; they were
not crossed at all. "Do ye na' ken ye're flyin' heer like a kite—wi' nae
mair than a threid holdin' ye?" He raised his muscular hands
and snapped an imaginary string between them. "We're all kites in
that wind," he said. And off he went into trance again.*
—MICHAEL MURPHY, GOLF IN THE KINGDOM

FALL 2008. SHEBOYGAN/KOHLER, WISCONSIN

A dozen of us gathered in the greater Kohler/Sheboygan Falls
area for a weekend in mid-October. The reason we had come
together was the Seamus MacDuff Fall Finale, an event named
for Shivas Irons's mysterious mentor, who lives in a cave off of
the thirteenth at Burningbush, and is owner of the famed baff-
ing spoon and author of the unpublished manuscript *Logarithms
of the Just: Bein' First Notes for a Physics o' the Spirit.*

I'd driven up on Friday evening, after briefly dropping in at
my father-in-law's sixty-fifth birthday party. Everyone wanted to

know where I was going and I had the rare privilege of explaining, "I'm playing in a golf tournament," followed by a pregnant pause, before adding, "for work."

The following morning I ate breakfast in my hotel room, then headed over to The Bull at Pinehurst Farms, a Jack Nicklaus–designed course carved out of a former dairy farm and offered as an alternative to the four mega–Pete Dye courses in nearby Kohler.

In the clubhouse I followed the arrow on the message board up to the second-floor meeting room where the Shivas Irons Society was going to convene. The walls of the staircase—and pretty much every room—were plastered with images of Jack. Young Jack. Fat Jack. LeRoy Neiman Jack. Celery soup diet Jack. 1986 Masters Champ Jack. Jack and Arnie. These images also had some overlap with the state of Wisconsin's most cherished form of artwork—pictures of Packers past and present. Thus, there was Jack with Vince Lombardi, which transitioned into Vince with just about anybody. All other empty wall space held a spotty mix of Bart Starr, Brett Favre, and Paul Hornung.

The meeting room was empty, but in the hallway I ran into a tall, bearded dentist named Jack, who—sensing my general cluelessness—quickly identified me as a wayward, first-time Fall Finale participant. He introduced himself and I explained that I was there to write a book. I found out that he was from Beaver Dam and had a handicap in the 10 to 13 range. Then, before I ran downstairs to grab a cup of coffee and he to the bathroom, Jack gave me a brief preview of the next forty-eight hours.

"Sometimes some really interesting shit happens," he said. "Other times it's just a golf weekend."

o o o o

About twenty minutes later the room was full—half of us sitting in comfy leather chairs and the rest on tall bar stools. We introduced ourselves, speaking briefly about why we were here, our experiences with golf, Shivas Irons, and any other free-form thoughts that seemed pertinent. There was Ray, a gentlemanly Texan in his mid-fifties, who—in a deep, but gentle voice—spoke with genuine reverence about the sport and his love of each and every one of its components: the outdoors, the clubs, the balls, and even the rules. A father and son from Chicago both discussed how it had brought their family together in new and interesting ways. A Milwaukee attorney named Peter talked about how he'd spent most of his life doing things at which he was remarkably capable. But golf allowed him the opportunity to experience ineptitude.

One common topic amongst the group was the difficulty in explaining the deeper aspects of golf (the themes of Murphy's and Pressfield's books, as well as any others that touched on the spiritual) to their golf buddies. Everyone wondered how one could help others see the Buddhism, the quantum physics, and the spiritual side of golf while standing on the first tee or riding in a cart without getting that telltale look that screamed "FREAK!!!"

Man after man said the following: "I've tried to persuade people for years, but now I've given up."

Looking around the room, I see a bunch of guys who are not freaks. They are neither fringe characters, nor are they out of the mainstream of American manhood. Each one will rush to the bar after the round, grab a beer or Scotch, and wait to see if Penn State beat Michigan, or how Wisconsin did against Iowa. There isn't one person here who doesn't pass in the real world. We are normal, but we are a subset, probably a fairly small one, that is completely comfortable in discussing golf within this context and not feeling like a lesser man.

This is underscored in dramatic fashion thirty minutes later when we go to the practice tee.

o o o o

After each of us has hit twenty to thirty balls, we are called together by Steve Cohen, the president, founder, and chief emissary of the Shivas Irons Society. Short, bearded, and in his late sixties, he is the Jewish Santa Claus of all that combines Ben Hogan and Bodhisattva.

With four or five corporate logo–shirted guys still hitting balls on the range, Cohen asks us to stand in a circle and hold hands. Without question. Without a moment's hesitation. Without anyone even appearing to be weirded out in the least, each of us grabs the hand of the man on each side.

Steve tells us to close our eyes and tune into our hearing. He asks us to hear that which is close and that which is far. Then we feel. We feel the wind. We notice its direction. Is it cooler than our skin?

By the time we begin to pay attention to the sun, I am breathing in and out—supremely relaxed, still awake two weeks after my return from Scotland. I can feel the sun disappear behind a large object that is either a cloud or the satellite holding all the · stuff that's been sucked out of Star Jones. I think to myself, "This is the only time I will feel *this sun;* this is the only time I will feel *this breeze.*"

As we conclude, Cohen asks us to concentrate on the circle, our connections to each other in the circle, and how that circle extends outwards into the world in whatever way that makes sense to each of us. We squeeze the hands of the men at our sides. And then we go back to hitting balls.

o o o o

The Fall Finale is a two-day event with a scoring system that takes the eighteen lowest scores we have over thirty-six holes and adjusts them for our handicap. Thus, if you birdie a par-5, it is worth the same as bogeying a par-3.

The other members of my foursome are Tad, a tall, energetic eye surgeon from Wasau with a 22-handicap and a penchant for dirty jokes; Jim, a mild-mannered family doctor from Green Bay with a long, smooth swing and a 12-handicap; and Peter, who despite his reasons for taking up the game has seemed to overcome his ineptitude and plays off of a 5-.

Everyone gets off the first tee nicely, but only Jim makes the green in regulation and pars. Tad and I bogey and Peter triples. On two, a dogleg right par-4, Peter and I both drop our drives in the drink, which I follow with a 5-iron into a deep bunker carved into the front left side of the elevated green. It takes me three shots to get out and I wind up with a 9.

What happened next was remarkably instructive. I am 6 over after two, standing on the tee of a 200-yard par-3 with a narrow entryway to the green. Peter hits first and blasts one past the pin that sticks on the green about 15 feet beyond. Jim, who parred the second as well, hits a nice shot that lands just short. Tad then gets up and swings like hell—which he does unapologetically. His fairway wood is headed for the left edge before it fades softly and sticks about 5 feet from the pin. I pull out my 5-wood as well and hit a nearly identical shot that lands inside of Tad's at 4 feet. I par and so does Peter. Jim bogeys and Tad rams his putt home for a birdie.

But what was important was this—as I counted up my score after two, I realized that the past was truly in the past. I could have had a ten or I could have had a birdie. It truly didn't matter. It might seem a stretch to say that it somehow helped me understand the concept of impermanence, but the truth is that it did.

I par the fourth, then bogey the fifth and sixth. The par-4 seventh is short, with an elevated green 280 yards from the tee, protected by a humongous and deep bunker set in a hill at about 240—with all errant drives finding forest on the left and the Onion River on the right. All of us stand there and wonder who the fuck thinks they could hit that green from the tee, but its mere existence is proof that hope springs eternal in those who play from the tips and claim a handicap that is probably ten strokes better than their actual game.

Everyone plays it safe. My 190-yard 5-wood is straight down the middle, leaving me 100 yards or so out, uphill, and into the wind. I pull out my 8-iron, which I miss a bit and send my ball flying over the left side of the trap. The shot was completely blind, but having seen the green from the tree, I hoped that I'd stayed right of the tree line and bounced toward the stick.

When I get up to the green, my ball is on the left fringe, 12 feet short of pin high. With a great feeling of calm, I go for it and my birdie putt falls in. I follow this by birdieing the eighth, a short par-5, where Tad persuades me to go for the green in two and I use my 3-wood to clear the green, leaving me 10 feet behind the putting surface in a clump of rough on a downward slope. Calmly, I chip to within 3 feet and hit my putt for a 4.

After getting greedy on the ninth, and paying for it with three shots to get out of another deep, patently insane green-side bunker, I play fairly well on the back, with some bogeys, a double, and a few pars. My best hole, however, is the 155-yard par-3 fifteenth.

It has been sunny and fairly warm all day. At least in relative terms. It is October in Wisconsin, so the low-60s feels like Palm Springs. But, on the fifteenth, the sun disappears behind some clouds and it becomes incredibly cold as a wind begins to blow directly at us, with a simultaneous cross breeze that shifts by the moment. This makes picking the appropriate club impossible—the result being that no one makes the green in regulation. I am 30 yards short and in the rough on the right. Then I hit my best shot of the day, a dead-handed knockdown pitch-chip that hits the fringe and rolls to a stop 5 inches from the cup.

Standing on the green, Peter, Jim, and Tad ask me for "the secret," which they are certain I have discovered—sand traps in Wisconsin aside—on my golf odyssey.

"I'll tell you after the hole," I say.

When the last of them holes out, Peter looks at me, "OK, come on—the secret."

I tell them about breaking 40 on the front nine at Hawks-head in southwestern Michigan during August. That day I was paired up with a retired lawyer who had an okay swing, hit the ball reasonably well, lacked distance, and was an unspectacular but steady putter.

After the front we grabbed a cup of coffee and watched the driving rain that would eventually keep us from finishing our round. I had a 38, going even par after doubling the first. I knew he'd been scoring pretty well and looked over at his card. He was 1 under. I thought about it and everything he recorded was accurate. He hadn't cheated one bit. But, good lord, I thought, how in the name of Jesus was he 1 under?

"Do you play like that often?" I asked.

"Sometimes," he said. "I'm about a 3-handicap."

He then explained that his wife had died five years earlier, shortly after he'd retired. A year later, he'd placed a personal ad looking for a woman interested in golf and a relationship. The woman who responded was a golf addict just like him and soon they were married. Each summer, he told me, they lived in Michigan, where they played golf every day—sometimes twice. In the fall, winter, and spring they were in Florida, where they played every day as well. It was the constancy, the repetition, the understanding of what one can and can't do that grew from playing so often that made breaking par a not so infrequent event.

"It evens things out," he said. "You just don't make stupid mistakes anymore. You don't three-putt often. You don't beat yourself. It just kind of becomes second nature."

Like any other discipline, I tell Peter, Jim, and Tad, if you do it every day and are patient—you become skilled. Yes, golf does require some talent and self-knowledge, and there are hacked up courses all over the world filled with retirees who play hundreds of rounds but rarely break 100. But, like achieving nirvana, playing every day becomes its own meditation. The score doesn't matter all that much. You attain mastery on some level and what matters is the playing.

o o o o

When we are done, Peter buys me a Guinness and we go outside so he can smoke a cigarette. Standing on the clubhouse deck, I see Scott, a tall, lean, tightly wound country lawyer with a great deadpan sense of humor. I ask how he did out there. Scott takes a drag off of his cigarette and a swig of Scotch before he says: "I needed someone out there to hold my hand."

I laugh.

Scott looks at me half-seriously. "I mean it."

o o o o

The motto of the Seamus MacDuff Fall Finale is that there is no bad weather for golf, only inappropriate clothing. Thus, on the morning of the second day, having read that there would be 30 to 40 mph winds blowing off the lake, I donned long underwear and three layers before heading out to Whistling Straits.

I drove about eight miles from my hotel in Kohler, past nothing but flatland farms in every direction. Then I saw Whistling Straits. Or rather, Whistling Straits emerged before me like some bizarre netherworld in which Peter Jackson had been asked to create a complex of über-expensive, Middle-Earth golf courses strategically located on the shores of Lake Michigan and as close as possible to one town famous for faucets and another for its bratwurst.

There are four Peter Dye courses located fairly close together in the Sheboygan/Kohler area. There are two at Whistling Straits—the Straits course and the Irish course. And at Blackwolf Run, there are a river course and a prairie course. Today we were playing the Straits.

I had seen pictures of all four courses online and was a bit awestruck. Those at Whistling Straits have been designed to recreate the traditional courses of Ireland and Scotland, complete with rolling topography, gigantic pot bunkers, and a flock of Scottish blackface sheep that grace a few fairways on the 7,514-yard Straits course, which had hosted the 2004 PGA Championship (won by Vijay) and where we would be playing on this blustery day. No picture, brochure, or course description, however, could prepare me for what was about to happen. Because, as I would come to realize, the Straits course is not a place where you play golf. Instead, it is something that happens to you.

The entrance to Whistling Straits is framed by a gigantic expanse of tall, soft, green mounds that go on and on. I suspect they are 10 to 12 feet high and appear to guard something other than a golf course. My first impression was that I might find some dairy-land Stonehenge once inside, or at the very least be greeted by mythical woodland creatures playing lutes and strumming harps.

Later, as we played, Jack and our caddie Craig both explained to me the efforts that went into transforming a flat bit of Wisconsin seashore into something so overwhelmingly Scots/Irish that it makes Gullane look like a $25 municipal course in Tulsa. Sand, they told me, had been hauled in 24/7 for seven months in order to create an effect that Jack sums up nicely on the sixth hole.

Standing before an insanely out of place and magnificent vista, the wind blowing his hair, he calls out, "This is Disneyland." This is underscored a few moments later when Tad asks the caddie, "Is it true that Dye overspent an unlimited budget?"

I cannot conceive of what it may have cost to build Whistling Straits or maintain it, but injecting a day or two of its operating costs into the market may well have been sufficient to solve the credit crisis of 2008.

Jack loves this pace with such genuine enthusiasm that during our windswept five-hour round, he patiently—like a Dodger fan being able to take his grandson back to Ebbets Field—takes me back to the pro tees on every hole so that I can see what the course is supposed to look like and explains where and how various events at the 2004 PGA unfolded in rich and compelling detail.

My other partners are Tad and Ken, a handsome, silver-haired retiree from Milwaukee who looks like an former member of Reagan's cabinet. It is Ken who brings the cigars and uses profanity the way that Chagall worked with stained glass.

On the first hole, I tee off last. Supremely relaxed I pull a 50-yard knuckleball left down a hill into some brown haylike grass. The caddie tells me to take another and I hit a nearly identical shot. From there, I manage a bogey, after a good 3-hybrid back onto the fairway and an 8-iron into the green. Then came the wind. And the traps.

I am a good bunker player. I am generally fearless and able to get out and do so effectively pretty much anywhere in the world, with the apparent exception of Kohler, Sheboygan, and the surrounding environs. At The Bull, I suspect that I lost nine shots in four traps. At the Straits it would be more of the same, because in their ardor to create a golfing experience that reflects the great courses in the world, Nicklaus and Dye apparently used a funhouse mirror to completely fuck me over with ridiculously deep bunkers, far worse than anything I saw during three rounds in Scotland.

I find the sand on the second hole, and take a quad. I'm not alone. Tad fares best with a 7, Jack has an 8, and Ken, the first of several X's.

"Fuck. Fuck. Fucking shit fuck," he moans.

I hit a bunker on each of the first four holes—and not only are all of them 5 to 10 feet below the fairway or green, but all have preposterously difficult lies. I am stuck in little crooks and corners, where I stand with one foot in, one foot out, with no clear path for my club to even reach the ball.

Much of the front nine is on the lake and the wind is beyond brutal. It's impossible to select a club. The third, a 163-yard par-3, plays as though it's at least 190 and all I can do is brave it and wait until we get to the middle holes to regain both the strokes and dignity that I've lost. Yet, amidst it all, with bogey being the best score any of us achieve on the first three, there is a sense of camaraderie. An hour ago, we were some guys thrown together in a foursome. Now, we are like mates in a foxhole. We are in this together and every marginally decent shot receives shouts of encouragement. As a group, we also begin to accept that our expectations will have to be adjusted.

On the fourth tee, the wind pushes my club involuntarily backwards as I prepare to swing. This moment takes me back to those halcyon days of August, when I lived in the low, low 80s.

In the midst of that exhilarating time, I sat watching the British Open as the wind made pro after pro miss fairway after fairway. And during that time, I actually had the following thought: "What the fuck is wrong with those guys? Jesus, just hit the fucking thing in the fairway." Now, God was paying me back— and I deserved it.

The fifth takes us away from the wind and water. A long par-5 that doglegs right around a pond, we play it as a silent hole—of sorts. My drive is nearly spectacular as it follows the layout perfectly, going straight 230 and then bending gently towards the corner. Then, it begins to fade more and more. I fear the water. Instead, I am in a waste bunker.

I take out my 4-hybrid and smoke one 180—into another waste bunker on the right. I grab my 8-iron. To aim at the heart of the green means carrying a pond on the left. Opting for right and hoping for the best, I hit a nice shot that would have finished pin high—had it not fallen into another bunker on the right, where I had the worst lie of my life, in a tiny corner, nearly surrounded by high lip and with no clear path to the green or even out of the sand. I walk around and around. I try innumerable stances. Then I decide to hit directly down and hope for a miracle.

After I slam down violently, my ball comes shooting out sideways, bounce off of a hill, then hard right, dying on the fringe. I two-putt and record the finest bogey I will ever have—three bunkers on a par-5.

I par the sixth with the wind behind me and nearly birdie the seventh with a tap-in par. After we hole out, Ken and I sit on a small hill, trying to light our cigars in the wind. He's a pro and has no problem. I am hunched, my head down over the flame, clicking and puffing like mad.

"Do me a favor," Ken says—looking like a million bucks. "Don't set your fucking balls on fire."

Jack heats up on the back, as does Tad. I am up and down. Ken suffers mightily.

As we head into fourteen and back into the wind, our caddie Craig says, "Welcome to the longest mile in golf." To help you understand the force of the wind, I will describe two events.

On fifteen, as Tad is about to hit a putt, his ball wavers on the green. The other caddie, giving him a line, explains that usually he would hit the ball in one spot, but with the wind he'd aim a bit further outside. "You've got to account for that wind," he says, as if we are holding drivers.

Later, walking up the next fairway, I am reminded of Steve Cohen explaining how he'd lain on the ground at the top of the cardiac hill at Gullane in a near monsoon and saw a flock of Russian Geese flying but not moving forwards. I laughed, assuming it was a tall tale. But, there, above me on fifteen, a seagull is trying to fly into the same headwind where we hit our tee shots. He flaps. He tries to catch a draft. He ducks a bit in hopes of getting under it. But, he never moves forward. I watch him try and try until he gives up, turns around, and lets the wind blow him to South Dakota. There's a Zen message in there somewhere.

The most remarkable hole at Whistling Straits is seventeen, which Dye has dubbed "Pinched Nerve." It's a 190-yard par-3, with the shores of Lake Michigan directly to your left. The green rises like a small mountain in the distance. In between—and far below—the path is strewn with traps and trouble of all kinds. There are few good options right of the green, and left there is the greatest hazard of all—a sheer 80-foot drop, with a few traps in the hillside to catch shots that almost make it before diving to a watery grave.

Standing on the tee, I decide to try a bit of "Fairways to Heaven" style nonattachment and hit one into the lake with no particular destination in mind. It's the longest, straightest drive I've hit in a month.

Pinched Nerve is playing as though it's 220 because of the wind and I pull out my 3-wood. I play for the left side, figuring that my ball will fade right as it almost always does. And I smoke it—my ball cutting right through the wind, high but strong. Straight as can be. It catches the left side of the green, pin high, takes one bounce and falls left, off the cliff into a bunker 35 feet below, cut into the side of the hill.

Tad and Ken both find themselves in trouble as well. But Jack crushes one that hits and sticks on the green.

When get to my ball I have a decent lie, but really have no physical, spiritual, or emotional framework for having to hit such a shot, which will need to fly sideways and directly upward over a castle wall of grass. Failing to execute this shot will only increase my misery—but there is no place for a safe bailout.

Tad stands on the edge, showing me where to aim. I clear my mind, settle down in my feet, loosen my hands, and just swing—with no fear. The ball sails up with a weird sliding trajectory, climbing upwards until it reaches where Tad stood moments ago.

I hear Tad screaming "great shot," while Jack and Ken clap and call out that my ball is safe. When I get to the top, I see that my shot wound up 5 feet past the apron on the right side, nestled in some thick rough. I chip on and two-putt for double. Yet I am exhilarated.

Moments later when Jack hits his birdie putt, I can see a broad smile on his usually restrained face. Like the rest of us, he has been enormously frustrated all day. A few holes before, I'd asked our caddie how many strokes this kind of wind adds. He told me that most people are lucky to be within 10 strokes of their handicaps.

Eighteen is a gigantic bitch of a par-4, but the wind is no longer a factor. The two-tiered fairway runs out about 240 yards before a 20-foot drop over a stream and onto one of two other fairways below. Like the rest of the course, it has an over-the-top quality, but when I am able to look at it from the perspective of the green it seems like a collaboration between Thomas Kincaid and J. M. Barrie.

Tad and I both hit huge drives that take us right to the end of the first fairway, just short of the drop-off. I am 170 from the pin and Tad is about 190. He hits first as Steve Cohen's group watches from behind the green. His 3-hybrid climbs and climbs and climbs, hits 12 feet before the pin and rolls left and closer to the hole, coming to a stop 6 feet out. Everyone applauds. Tad is ecstatic. He pars, Jack and I bogey. Ken takes an 8. We all shake hands.

"Let's get a fucking drink," Ken says to all of us.

o o o o

Inside, it's warm. I have a beer, and am soon joined by Jim, Peter, Scott, and Jack. We sit at the bar watching the Packers play the

Colts. Earlier this morning Peter and I had sat with Jim, who was despondent about his game and bemoaning all that befell him after the third hole. He tells me that he wished his backswing was as short and compact as mine. I tell him that I wish mine was as long and fluid as his. But mostly we talk him down, explaining that everyone goes through these phases when their game is in transition.

Then I am reminded of dinner the night before, which Jim had missed because it was his anniversary. Before we all walked out into the cool night air, Steve Cohen offered a toast straight from Shivas Irons.

"Fuck our ever getting better."

Everyone drank and then roared with delight.

Later, in my hotel room, I looked up that passage in the book, which I have read several times, but lack the encyclopedic knowledge of most of my fellow society members. I found it on pages 185 and 186, in part two of the book, after the essential story is over and in a section where Murphy discusses various concepts brought to light by his time with Shivas.

"Tae enjoy yersel', that's the thing," Shivas says, "and beware the quicksands o' perfection."

And that is exactly what Peter and I tell Jim. Don't try too hard. Don't think too much. Enjoy the game. That's what it's there for. That's what I've learned.

o o o o

Steve Cohen calls us into the Player's Room just off the bar, where Steve Proudman, the stocky, energetic guy who organized the event, is sitting at a long wooden table with his tam-o'-shanter in front of him. He is red-faced from the wind.

After a few comments, he gets to the tournament results, something that I'd completely forgotten about since we made the turn the day before. Fourth place goes to Jack. I can't remember third. But, much to my surprise I am in second, with a two-day, best-eighteen-holes adjusted score of 63.

Sitting there I begin to realize that Tad must have won. There is a moment of dramatic pause and Proudman says that indeed, Tad's 61 puts him in first place. Tad is beaming—a grown man with the joy of a young one, beating a room full of guys at a difficult game.

They take Tad's photograph and explain that his name will be on a plaque that features a hickory-shafted club and hangs in the Player's Room at a place where both he and Vijay have been declared champions.

Watching him I feel something unfamiliar. Though not accustomed to winning tournaments of any kind during my forty-two years, I realize that I've never been so happy to finish second to someone in my life.

o o o o

The Seamus MacDuff Fall Finale was the end of my journey and finishing in second place was somehow symbolic—I had come a long way, but I wasn't completely there. And I was okay with that.

During the course of this odyssey, my golf game had improved immeasurably. The tangible evidence was that my handicap had dropped from 18 to 11. While seven strokes may not seem like a colossal sea change, they are fairly significant. I did not break 80, but I shot it a few times and was under 40 for nine for the first time in my life, and then repeated it often enough that it became unspectacular, yet retained all of the good feelings that it originally inspired. I know that someday, with enough practice, I will get under 80 and bring my handicap into the single digits. But those things are also far less important to me now.

Instead, what I took away were the many things that I learned, from getting abstract to swinging from my feet and drawing up the energy from the earth; from loosening my grip to breathing my way through difficult times and bad shots; from playing swing, rather than working, golf to not keeping score; from listening to the course to accepting that 80 may be the best score I ever shoot. Okay. I'm still working on that last one. Most importantly, my swing became a source of pleasure, which more often than not brought my scores closer to par. All of these things brought a joy to my game that exceeds anything I might achieve on the golf course.

As far as my anxiety and general sense of ennui, that changed as well. Being fully awake did not last indefinitely. A week or so after the Seamus MacDuff event, I began to feel less present—started grasping to regain what I thought I'd found in Scotland. I have not achieved nirvana, nor did I become the carefree Bing Crosby I had hoped would ultimately emerge. But I still love cardigans and am no longer frightened to smoke a pipe for fear it will give me cancer—even if it will, or won't. How Zen is that?

I became much more at ease with myself and did shed quite a bit of that inner Woody Allen. My anxiety still exists, but it is smaller and gets more so with the passage of time. I did not attain satori, but I now believe it exists and have touched it—if only for a few weeks in October 2008. But no longer am I trapped in the sands of perfection. I try too hard and think too much on occasion, but the most important thing is that I do my best to meditate every day.

Both my inner life and my golf game remain works in progress. But when I think about where I was and how far I've come, I am reminded of the Zen proverb "Before enlightenment: chop wood, carry water. After enlightenment: chop wood, carry water."

Thus, that is what I will continue to do—chopping my wood and carrying my water. Some people do it in an ashram, others in church. I do it by playing golf.

o o o o

After we all congratulated Tad, most of us headed to the bar for another drink. About twenty minutes later, I said my goodbyes. Peter, with whom I'd established a strong connection despite barely knowing each other, gave me a big hug. I slapped Tad on the back, then shook hands with Ken and Jack. I thanked Steve Proudman for organizing the event. I found Steve Cohen by the fire and thanked him as well.

A second before I left the bar, I looked back at everyone and sensed the impermanence of the moment—accepting that we may play together every year or that I may never see them again. That weekend was that weekend. It will never happen again, just as I would never feel that same sun, or that same wind on my face, or re-hit my tee shot on seventeen aiming further to the right. And I know that is the reality of golf, of life—and of that moment, which combined the two. The best I could do—could ever do—was be present.

But, most of all, I thought back on the group I'd just left and was filled with a sense that these are my people.

ACKNOWLEDGMENTS

I would like to thank the following people without whose time, patience, and skill this book would never have been written.

Jonathan Lyons of Lyons Literary who understood the idea for this book immediately and helped it find the perfect home. Emily Haynes at Chronicle Books, a great editor who saved me from myself on a few occasions and whose insights made this book all the better. I also owe thanks to Matt Robinson, formerly of Chronicle, for seeing the potential in this book and for his belief that I could pull it off. Also at Chronicle: Emilie Sandoz, Mark Burstein, Becca Cohen, Jacob Gardner, and Beth Steiner. In addition, I would also like to thank the great Charlie Schroeder, the Ojai Valley Resort and Spa, and Michele Szynal at Callaway Golf.

On this journey I met, worked, and hacked up courses with a group of people who made me remember that camaraderie is indeed the best part of this game or any game. These folks include: Yoni Zaluski at Whole Body Golf; Steven Yellin at Perfect Mind/ Perfect Motion; Doc Parent and Ken at Zen Golf; Jim Waldron at Balance Point Golf School; Printer Bowler; Bill and Coach Stephen at Renegade Mental Golf; the Golf Sensei—Jamie Zimron; Les Bolland and Dennis at SwingGolf; Rabbi Joshua Strulowitz and Tony; Abbot John; Andrew Greig; Vin Harris of Fairways to Heaven; Mahadeva Ishaya of Golf in the Moment; and finally, the members of the Shivas Irons Society and the men of the 2008 Seamus MacDuff Fall Finale, most especially Steve Cohen, Steve Proudman, Peter, Jim, Tad, Jack, Scott, and Ken. I thank you all.

My family put up with some prolonged absences as their dad/husband "worked" on this book, flying all over the place taking exotic golf lessons, shaving strokes from his handicap and playing with interesting people. Thus I owe a great deal to my wife Susan and my sons William, Leo, Teddy, and Francis—for their patience and love.

Additionally, I would like to thank the rest of my family (Mom, Dad, Jer, Sandy, John, Ro, Kate, Frank, Shamus, and Clancy), and my semi-regular golf partners (Tim, Dave, Bob, Billy, AJ, Phil, and Dr. A) for their friendship and support.

Finally, I would like to thank Michael Murphy and Steven Pressfield whose wonderful books not only created a genre, but also caused some unlikely folks (myself included) to examine and challenge our preconceptions about life.